MW00345866

RICHARD E. MYERS LECTURES

Presented by University Baptist Church, Charlottesville

REV. DR. MATTHEW A. TENNANT, EDITOR

MAKING THE WORLD OVER

*Confronting Racism,
Misogyny, and Xenophobia
in U.S. History*

R. MARIE GRIFFITH

UNIVERSITY OF VIRGINIA PRESS

Charlottesville and London

University of Virginia Press
© 2021 by the Rector and Visitors of the University of Virginia
All rights reserved
Printed in the United States of America on acid-free paper

First published 2021

9 8 7 6 5 4 3 2 1

Library of Congress Cataloging-in-Publication Data

Names: Griffith, R. Marie (Ruth Marie), author.
Title: Making the world over : confronting racism, misogyny, and
    xenophobia in U.S. history / R. Marie Griffith.
Other titles: Confronting racism, misogyny, and xenophobia in U.S. history
Description: Charlottesville : University of Virginia Press, 2021. | Series:
    Richard E. Myers Lectures | Includes bibliographical references and
    index.
Identifiers: LCCN 2020051379 (print) | LCCN 2020051380 (ebook) |
    ISBN 9780813946344 (hardcover) | ISBN 9780813946351 (ebook)
Subjects: LCSH: Xenophobia—United States—Historiography. |
    Racism—United States—Historiography. | Misogyny—United States—
    Historiography. | United States—Race relations—Historiography. |
    United States—Ethnic relations—Historiography. | Minorities—United
    States—Social conditions. | National characteristics, American.
Classification: LCC E184.A1 G892 2021 (print) | LCC E184.A1 (ebook) |
    DDC 305.800973—dc23
LC record available at https://lccn.loc.gov/2020051379
LC ebook record available at https://lccn.loc.gov/2020051380

Cover photo: "Women should take part, we are all part of this."
(iStock/Tassii)

For those honest enough to confront the failures of the past, unquiet enough to seek justice in the present, and brave enough to make the world over

We made the world we're living in and we have to make it over.

—James Baldwin, "Notes for a Hypothetical Novel: An Address"

We are all always awash in each other's lives, and for most of us that shared life, recorded as history, will be the only artifact we leave behind.

—Danielle Allen, *Talking to Strangers: Anxieties of Citizenship since* Brown v. Board of Education

CONTENTS

MAKING THE
WORLD OVER

INTRODUCTION

What Can We Do?

What can we do?

This question, often asked in a tone of desperation if not despair, is one that audiences around the United States over more than a decade have repeatedly asked, following the many lectures on religion and politics I've given at colleges and universities, religious and civic organizations, and other public gatherings. Needless to say, most people are not seeking easy answers so much as pleading aloud for ways to help improve the civic and political culture of the United States and end certain types of suffering or injustice. Whether our discussions have focused on religious intolerance, gender inequality, structural racism, regulations on sexuality, the country's broken immigration system, the abuse of authority by political and religious elites, voter suppression, or court battles over abortion, American observers have shown

1

themselves to be keenly concerned about the state of this nation, distraught over what they view as the horrors unleashed or exacerbated by Donald Trump's presidential administration both before and during the COVID-19 pandemic, and eager to do something constructive to mitigate them. They acutely want, in other words, to *make the world better*. I expect other public speakers from a range of fields—academia, journalism, the legal profession, and more—have experienced the same longing from audience members fighting a sense of helplessness, some wrestling with their own naiveté or complicity. Knowing my own lecture hall answers have been halting and painfully insufficient, this book of essays offers what I hope is a more articulate and viable response.

"Making the world better" is, however, a lofty goal, and projects that seem promising often prove to be paradoxical. No scene better illustrates the need for caution than one from *The Handmaid's Tale,* Margaret Atwood's celebrated dystopian novel. Commander Fred Waterford—a man who helped establish the Republic of Gilead, a totalitarian theonomy founded on the ruthless subjugation of women—tries to explain to his captive and maltreated handmaid Offred why he worked to upend so brutally relations between women and men. In the televised adaption of this scene, he goes further to describe the savage mutilation of one handmaid discovered to be a lesbian—a grave crime in this patriarchal world. Seeing Offred's anguish, he defends himself and his fellows for ousting American democracy in this new state, saying, "We only wanted to make the world better." "*Better?*" Offred splutters in livid disbelief. Coldly, the Commander rejoins, "Better never means better for everyone. It always means worse for some."[1]

U.S. history, it must be remembered, is filled with examples of ostensibly well-intentioned efforts to make the world better that, in retrospect, many judge to have been good only for the few and profoundly destructive to many others. The history of indigenous nations in this country is one looming example that is far too frequently buried below the ground from which non–Native Americans narrate the past. From the outset, we must acknowledge that the founding of the United States was not simply the product of the Revolutionary War, especially the war as romanticized in numberless books, paintings, and productions. The conditions leading up to that war could occur only after long years of settler colonialism became naturalized, part of the ongoing violent process of dispossessing native inhabitants of their land and assuming control over geographies and natural resources that were once home to untold numbers of indigenous people, many of whom the white settlers destroyed with disease, poverty, broken treaties, and war. Settlers no doubt believed they were making the world better for themselves and their kin and kind, but they either did not perceive or did not care about the awful price paid by others for white self-improvement.

Closer to our own time, other examples of mixed consequences abound: urban renewal efforts to improve cities have displaced hundreds of thousands of people over the years, predominantly people of color. The GI Bill distributed benefits to veterans of World War II in radically unequal terms that also overwhelmingly affected African Americans, who were turned away from efforts to buy homes in suburbs redlined to be "whites only." Humanitarian efforts of many kinds, including Christian missions, have had negative effects on many of the people they purportedly aimed to help. And U.S. military interventions into the Arab world premised on such notions as saving Muslim women from oppression have resulted in countless deaths of innocent people. All of these efforts, and many others, were backed by people claiming to improve the standing order and professing their own innocent good intentions, reminding us that any assertion about ways of "making the world better" demands scrutiny of the interested parties behind it and the lives they actually hope to improve. Whose lives, that is, *matter?*

No thinker has probed these problems more deeply than James Baldwin, one of the greatest writers of the twentieth century. Throughout his astonishing oeuvre and public lectures, Baldwin called Americans to account for their long habit of forgetting inconvenient truths about the past. In particular, he called white Americans to account for the hypocrisy of what Baldwin's latest interpreter, Eddie Glaude Jr., simply calls "the lie," the myth white people have perpetually insisted upon that they are innocent and pure of heart and ever kind to others. The whitewashing of history to strip it from all unpleasantness and unjust, abusive violence toward others has created conditions that have worked to make the world better for a selection of the country's inhabitants and worse for many others (far more than "some"). In a successfully whitewashed history, the past is quickly forgotten, both its beautiful parts and its evils. We Americans, Baldwin warned, are historical amnesiacs, suffering from a type of dementia that leaves white and Black people alike bereft of both past and future; all has been reduced to survival of the fittest in the now, and the nation will not long survive its own atrocities. Force yourselves to witness the consequences of complacent ignorance, he demanded: how will you now guard against history's destruction and your own? The challenge, he wrote in one form or another over and over again, was "attempting to tell as much of the truth as one can bear, and then a little more." Only by facing the past as well as the present could a better world and future emerge.[2]

But in fact Baldwin was not content with the aim of making the world *better;* he called us to do much more than that. "We made the world we're living in," he warned, "and we have to make it over."[3] *Making the world over* is a more audacious, more challenging, and possibly more foolhardy goal than making it moderately better. But our collective senility, exacerbated by a grossly underestimated and mishandled pandemic, has brought us to the brink of what seems to many a near collapse of American institutions, political stability, and societal life. Wait much longer, and it may be too late to rescue the norms and practices worth saving, much less improve them in piecemeal fashion. Frankly, I see little choice other than to commit what efforts we can to making our world over in the sense that Baldwin meant, starting with confronting the hardest truths of our own history.

How to discern and preserve the lessons of history is indeed a question of perennial importance and a strikingly urgent one today, as we see repeatedly in our era's recurring conflicts over public monuments and historical statues: who gets to be the hero in our shifting narrative of the country's past? The very telling of history itself is routinely challenged by what has come to be called "fake news." The *Oxford English Dictionary* traces that term back to an 1890 newspaper article, whereas the historian Sarah Churchwell associates it with President Woodrow Wilson's 1915 "America First" speech and his warnings against "the rumors of irresponsible persons" and "coteries where sinister things are purposed" to undermine the nation.[4] "Fake news" gained widespread usage during Trump's 2016 presidential election campaign, in Churchwell's words, "undergoing a remarkable reversal from a charge levied against him for his brazen lies, distortions and fabrications, to a complaint he turned on his accusers, claiming that any unflattering fact about him was just 'fake news.'"[5] Others, however, have seen a proliferation of "fake news" across mass media and the internet in some of the very sources Trump would claim to be true (Infowars, Rush Limbaugh, various personalities on Fox News, etc.). As an increasingly splintered digital media landscape has transformed the ways in which people absorb information about just about everything, finding reliable sources and voices to trust has become an exceedingly fraught venture.

Discerning history is, then, a more vital task than ever in the early decades of the twenty-first century, when much of the world's population still lives under tyrannical government powers that censor their access to information about the past as well as the present. It is not only dictatorships or would-be dictatorships that enact such censorship, however; republics do it too, and if their methods must be subtler than dictatorial decrees and government-censored textbooks, they are greatly aided by the efforts of elites who gain advantage from the historical ignorance of the masses. These issues have been much on the minds of many Americans unnerved by the fact that the populace holds such contrary views about *which* sources peddle fake news. It's confusing to sort out: as the philosopher Harry Frankfurt wryly put it in his meditation on the subject, "One of the most salient features of our culture is that there is so much bullshit."[6]

This, then, is the context in which I have tried in these pages to give one scholar's partial answer to the pressing question shared by so many Americans: *What can we do?* While the American polarization so often decried in recent years is really not new—hostile disagreement and conflict have been part of our fabric from the start—Trump's presidency truly bombarded us with an unusually dramatic series of crises, from whatever outlets we consult: immigrant parents and children separated from one another at the U.S.-Mexican border and caged in monstrous conditions, with little medical care and no plan for family reunification; restrictions on travelers and international visitors from Muslim-majority countries; Russian espionage and interference in U.S. elections, met with indifference by the Trump administration; systemic sexual abuse; an unconscionably high death toll from the coronavirus boosted by the administration's greed and magical thinking; and more. But by no means is this the first era in U.S. history when the surrounding world felt perilous. One cannot name a decade over the past half century, or any time in the nation's past, when some or many Americans did not fear for their safety and for the future of the country; fears of this nature have clouded many minds and pervaded people's lives throughout history. Whether perceived threats from abroad or alleged internal threats to the nation, the terrors of violence against women and people of color or dread of the wholesale collapse of democracy, fear has been a perennial undercurrent of our history. Witness the January 6, 2021, storming of the U.S. Capitol by extremists claiming the 2020 election was stolen from Trump. President Biden inherited the legacy of these fears. So did we.[7]

Even if we came fully to understand all of our cultural and social rifts and why they feel so bitter in the early decades of the twenty-first century, as so many experts across a range of fields have tried to do, it is a tall order to imagine inducements for reacting productively in the hope of making the world better for more than just a very small "some." But it's crucial to make the effort nonetheless. As the political scientist Danielle Allen so eloquently writes in *Talking to Strangers,* "We are all always awash in each other's lives": so how can we think more purposefully about that shared life and how to live it?[8] In the end, I have tried here to address some of what appear to be the most critical issues dividing Americans over time, consider the imperative to confront them, and deliberate on a few of the values we might cultivate in purposeful ways so as to address these issues most usefully.

To be clear, I am not an ethicist or a philosopher or a theologian or clergyperson, nor any other sort of moral theorizer from whom we more typically hear about the values I discuss in these pages. Rather, I am a historian of American religion who has for some years dug into various conflicts within our country's past, especially those pertaining to gender, sexuality, and religion, and who has tried to think deeply about why these conflicts and others—particularly race and, if less visibly, class—remain so unresolved and bitter today. There are most assuredly vast literatures on all of the subjects I cover in these essays, and numerous thinkers who have influenced my own thinking; many appear in the endnotes, highlighting the fact that whatever contributions I make here are part of a wide-ranging conversation that long predates me and will far outlive me too. I'm also aware that most Americans outside of small intellectual circles do not read those literatures and may not have access to many of them, nor are they primarily interested in scholarly arguments about them. My aim with this book is not so much to engage in debate with my tribe of scholars (though I'll certainly be pleased if it is of interest to them) but to analyze some of the burning conflicts that, while rooted in much older historical encounters, events, and legal rulings, today seem ripe to inspire revolt and tear the country asunder. It is to speak candidly to students, nonspecialists, and general readers who care about the state of the United States and the world in the twenty-first century and who may be fighting a sense of helplessness about how to make things better.

The first chapter, "Truth," reflects on the legacies of slavery in the United States and perennial conflicts over telling that history and teaching it to new generations of Americans. Which historical truths, or versions of history, does one tell? Is it disrespectful, or unpatriotic, to continue talking about slavery all these years after Emancipation, as many white people seem to believe; or is the opposite the case—that to minimize or ignore our nation's slaveholding past is less about loving the country than about sentimentalizing a fantasy of white innocence, an offense to those who suffered under the slavery system and to their descendants? The founding paradox of the United States—what the sociologist Gunnar Myrdal called the "American Dilemma"—is that the writers of the Declaration of Independence supported slavery even as they asserted that "all men are created equal" and claimed that humans were endowed with three "unalienable rights" that enslaved humans could not access: "life, liberty, and the pursuit of happiness." The Founding Fathers deepened this paradox in the nation's governing document, the Constitution, by permitting slavery and tolerating the continued importation of captured foreign persons for twenty more years. The long-term effects of these early events have roiled the American people throughout our history, and the question of how to respond to this reality is as contentious today as it has ever been. Because the whitewashing of slavery and racism is chiefly perpetuated by whites, this chapter aims itself especially at white readers but is very much intended to be useful for nonwhite readers as well.

The second chapter, "Empathy," turns to immigration policy and our nation's long series of arguments over which foreigners should be welcomed into our borders and offered a path to citizenship. In the history of U.S. immigration, does one empathize with the immigrant or with the border agent patrolling the entry of foreigners? What of the unemployed citizen who sees the immigrant as a threat to his or her own well-being? Is it possible to empathize with more than one party in this debate, or does that show weakness, complicity, or both? Both federal policies and social attitudes toward migrants and would-be settlers in the United States have vacillated wildly over the centuries, and the conflicts currently roiling the nation have numerous precedents. This chapter wrestles with the critical question of what the nation's stance on immigrant people says about who Americans are.

Chapter 3, "Courage," explores the nation's long struggle over gender roles and the persistent entrenchment of misogyny. By misogyny, I do not mean a raw feeling of hatred toward all women; rather, following the conceptual framework set forth by the philosopher Kate Manne, it is a system of enforcing hierarchical gender norms by exacting severe costs from women who flout them, especially by withholding (or appearing to withhold) the caregiving disproportionately expected for women to devote to men and children. How has misogyny structured our society over time, and to what degree have we failed to reckon with its effects? How much courage does it take for women to break with deep expectations of compliance, and for male allies to encourage and support them in doing so? This chapter concludes by looking at recent electoral politics to analyze the role that misogyny plays in our nation today.

The fourth chapter, "Conversation," shifts direction to examine a controversy that ties in to all three of the previous chapters' subjects: the country's protracted debates over women's reproductive rights. Enslaved women were raped and forced to bear their owners' children, who then became enslaved themselves, and the owners' property; those women had virtually no control over their reproductive capacities. Immigrant women have often reaped the disgust of white Americans for ostensibly bearing too many children, and many underwent forced sterilization on U.S. soil: California alone, the nation's "most zealous sterilizer," which carried out the highest number of eugenic sterilizations in the United States between 1909 and 1979 (twenty thousand out of approximately sixty thousand in thirty-two states), targeted Mexican American women at highly disproportionate rates, coding their offspring as "delinquent, socially deviant, and more prone to feeblemindedness than 'American children.'"[9] And finally the long struggle over misogyny in the United States has often centered on reproductive rights, from access to basic information about birth control to laws governing maternity leave and job security for pregnant women and mothers, as well as the regulation of legal abortion. Today, it is abortion that roils us most, and I try to attend to the complexity of recognizing conscience claims on all sides and deliberating on them together through deeper conversation across ideological lines. What are the possibilities of conversation, and what are its limits? Can one converse authentically without unduly compromising one's own values?

The conclusion, "Small Promptings for Making the World Over," tries to address in print the "what can we do?" question that I and countless other public speakers have received over and over again in public settings, as we've given talks at colleges, universities, congregations, and civic spaces around the country, as well as in private discussions, small-group conversations, and classroom debates. With that question, people are asking what practices and habits they can cultivate in order to address our country's deep problems of injustice and polarization. At a historical moment where so many people seem to feel dismayed, disillusioned, and fearful about the state of our nation, it is urgent that we seek common ground, not for the sake of the nation or nationalism but for the sake of our humanity and participation in a global community. I've tried to do a deep dive into these issues and welcome reactions, critiques, and further suggestions from readers who wish to communicate with me.

Gilead is not a world I ever want to live in. But as philosophers and historians have warned for centuries, it only takes a small army to bring about a totalitarian social order, so long as the majority of the public is indifferent to or ignorant of its possibility. Both *The Handmaid's Tale* and the sequel that followed thirty-five years later, *The Testaments,* repeatedly illuminate this truth as well. And reading Baldwin alongside the story of Gilead reminds me that, while I may feel a deep kinship with Offred and the other handmaids in this story, I am a comfortably situated middle-class white woman who surely looks much more like the Commander's complicitous, enslaving, sadistic wife to those with less privilege and fewer social advantages than I have, those whose lives have been injured by evils my eyes have missed or have refused to see. There are most certainly authoritarian features to my own world from which I am largely exempt, but which have deeply damaging effects on others. Ultimately, then, these reflections on history are intended to be ethical in nature, to suggest some ways of addressing the questions that many are already asking in striving to understand the conflicts driving the United States today and the past that has brought us to this present.

"Better" should not have to mean "worse for some," whatever Commander Waterford says and however much social and political programs of alleged betterment have incorporated savagery toward those perceived to be standing in the way. At the very least, it is wrong to be so complacently nonchalant about, much less complicit in, such barbarity. An indispensable part of defeating both complacence and complicity is cultivating the steady habit of facing history and telling "as much of the truth as one can bear, and then a little more," in service to trying to make the world over. Innumerable people from countless walks of life are attempting to do just that, and with this small book of essays I make my latest effort to join them.

1

TRUTH

Legacies of Slavery and
How to Tell History

Not everything that is faced can be changed; but nothing
can be changed until it is faced.
—James Baldwin, "As Much Truth as One Can Bear"

THE STANDARD EARLY AMERICAN historical narrative that most
white children learn in school has traditionally been one of benevolent white people—"Pilgrims"—crossing the ocean from England
and enjoying a delicious communal meal with the generous, if
primitive, native peoples they encountered here. Their arrival in
1620 is what most Americans have been taught to consider the
first "real" settlement in what would become the United States,
thereby overlooking not only the English settlers who came to
Jamestown, Virginia, in 1607, but the indigenous Americans
("Indians") who had very much already settled much of the land,
as well as the settlers from other parts of Europe who came here
before the British. I don't think I have to persuade you of this fact;
the myth of the First Thanksgiving as the beginning of American

The First Thanksgiving 1621, Jean Leon Gerome Ferris, ca. 1915. Oil painting, from a series titled *The Pageant of a Nation*. (Universal History Archive/Getty Images)

history is deeply interwoven into the white American collective memory.

Most people learn, at later stages of education, that this glossy image is far from the realities of colonial encounter; indeed, high school textbooks in many parts of the country, and still more college and university history courses, do work to unmask the heroic legends and tell truer stories about the violence against indigenous people that enabled European colonists to occupy lands that others long considered their home. Many learn eventually, if vaguely, about the Native Americans who, when the colonists could not win them over to be helpful trading partners or of some other use, were massively displaced and many slaughtered, with wounding effects that persist to this day. And some learn about the long history of American slavery, though hazily and many distances removed from its full horrors.

To my fellow white Americans: Most of us did not learn some basic facts in school, and our ignorance has had pernicious effects. To readers of color, especially Americans of African descent: It is likelier than not that your own U.S. history curricula were also inadequate and that the cost of being misled by what you were taught has been high, up to and including what Frantz Fanon called "internalization or rather epidermalization of . . . inferiority."[1] Education, that is, is a formidable tool of subjugation because it deforms the identity and consciousness of both powerful and colonized people in an effort to persuade people of color to accept the racial status quo and assume that their position in society is the order of nature. Countless children the nation over have received inadequate schooling in U.S. history, so let me start with a few basic facts about one subect in particular, which is slavery and its aftermath:

According to the best estimates scholars have collected from shipping records and assembled into the Trans-Atlantic Slave Trade Database, approximately 12.5 million African persons were sent to the New World between 1525 and 1866, the years of the slavery trade. The Middle Passage was so hazardous that roughly 12 percent of them died aboard ship before reaching the New World. Roughly 10.7 million people did survive the terrible journey to be enslaved in North America, the Caribbean, and South America. About 450,000 native Africans were transported into North America, either directly from Africa or after landing first in the Caribbean. Although infant and child mortality rates in North America were high due to undernourishment, enslaved persons' offspring—who were considered the property of the enslaved's owners—led to millions more being enslaved here. By the time the nation went to war over slavery in 1861, according to the federal census, well over three million people were enslaved in the United States.[2]

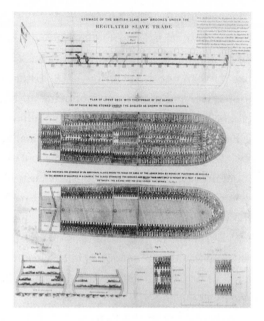

"Stowage of the British slave ship *Brookes* under the regulated slave trade act of 1788." (Library of Congress, Prints and Photographs Division, LC-USZ62-44000)

These are straightforward numbers, undisputed by experts as far as I know, but they were not part of many white people's education for well over a century after slavery was abolished in the United States in 1865. But times have been changing. Many efforts to tell this history, and to more generally tell the fuller truths of colonial conquest and settlement as well as the aftermath of segregation and racism, have appeared over the past thirty years or so and have made a difference to countless numbers of American students and readers, and Americans generally. This approach has sometimes been called "revisionist history," because it challenges and revises old assumptions about history with new or newly rediscovered evidence. It reinterprets the past for the sake of veracity and sometimes alters observers' assessments of what to celebrate and what to lament.

For instance, U.S. historians have come to understand that ideologies of racism and racial hierarchy were developed to justify the enslavement of Blacks by whites. These included actual theologies: that is, throughout much of U.S. history, most white Christians have firmly believed that God had designed the racial makeup of the world and that he intentionally made them unequal. This was part of God's racially ordered plan. During the centuries of enslavement, white Christians who supported the slavery system (whether they owned any persons or not) mostly took for granted that biblical references to slavery meant that enslaving Africans was perfectly moral, authorized by God. White Christians interpreted the story of Noah in the book of Genesis to suggest that God had cursed Ham, Noah's son, and all who were begotten by him through the generations, who were thought to be those with black skin.[3] Subjugation of Blacks to whites was the result, justifying not only slavery but racial inequality and segregation of the races more broadly. Religion, in short, was a fundamental support structure for racism and enslavement: according to the theology of segregationism, God had created separate and discrete races, and He intended them to stay that way. Knowing this now, white Christians have to take this history into account when exploring the past, rather than imagining that the racists were people wholly unlike themselves, or that their religion has somehow been pure from any complicitous role in the fortresses of slavery, segregation, inequality, and white nationalism.[4]

It's easy to see how this sort of revisionist history can make some people feel anxious. Learning that political heroes, such as the nation's Founding Fathers, held views that many today find abhorrent is difficult, sometimes even painful. And it can feel quite personal; as Robin DiAngelo puts it, describing the "white fragility" that many white people experience around the subject of race, "the mere suggestion that being white has meaning often triggers a range of defensive responses. These include emotions such as anger, fear, and guilt and behaviors such as argumentation, silence, and withdrawal."[5] Some become so indignant at the message that leaders like Thomas Jefferson weren't saints that they rail against the messenger for ruining something precious to them. That, in fact, is what has happened in these decades of revisionist history: a number of white writers with public platforms have felt personally assaulted by the findings and new interpretations of progressive historians, and they have gone on the attack in turn.

The backlash to revisionist accounts of U.S. history has been fierce. One historian recounted telling friends at church that he taught at a university and typically hearing a response like, "Bless your heart—it must be awful working in the midst of all those revisionists!"[6] In some conservative circles, "awful" seems to be a common view of what goes on in universities generally, and the academic humanities, in particular. The antirevisionist reaction has been shaped by celebrity pundits and politicians such as Rush Limbaugh, Pat Buchanan, George Will, Lynne Cheney, and Newt Gingrich, all of whom have lambasted such nontraditional (by their standards) historical subfields as women's history, labor history, and African American, Hispanic American, Asian American, and Native American history. In what the historian Gary Nash has called "his wildly ahistorical book," *To Renew America,* Gingrich blames historians and "cultural elites" for undermining American culture by working to (these are Gingrich's own words) "discredit [American] civilization and replace it with a culture of irresponsibility that is incompatible with *American freedoms as we have known them.*" The first task in restoring America is "to return to teaching Americans about America and teaching immigrants how to become Americans." For Gingrich American history is thus: "From 1607 until 1965," he writes, "America had one continuous civilization built around a set of commonly accepted legal and cultural principles. From the Jamestown colony and the Pilgrims, through Tocqueville's 'Democracy in America,' up to the Norman Rockwell paintings of the 1940s and 1950s, there was a clear sense of what it meant to be an American."[7]

This conflict exemplifies a profound moral and political problem that has long divided the people of the United States: the way we talk, or do not talk, about our nation's history, and particularly the history of slavery and all of its legacies that remain with us still. Far from being a simple matter of sticking to the proverbial facts, history-telling is an interpretive act loaded with assumptions, and a political act too; some themes must be emphasized while others are not, and the history-teller's favorite characters are often whitewashed. While not simply a matter of conservative versus progressive approaches to U.S. history—liberals are prone as well to whitewashing their own—there is an important moral distinction to be drawn in terms of approaches that overlook inconvenient truths about unjust violence being perpetrated against whole peoples within history's purview. This chapter seeks to confront the apparent opposition between two starkly different approaches to history, made unambiguously visible through the lens of slavery and race.

The type of history to which Gingrich wanted to return is one with a lengthy history of its own. As Abram Van Engen most recently lays out, the classic historical narrative that celebrated virtuous, persecuted, freedom-loving Pilgrims as the real "founders" and guiding lights of American civilization arose in early nineteenth-century New England. It completely erased the Spanish and French explorers who first set foot here—they were violent "conquerors," whereas the Pilgrims and the Puritans were virtuous "colonists"—and thrust Native Americans into the savage backwoods, emerging only for occasional friendly trading with their white neighbors. It relegated slavery to the South (despite the very real history of the North, including New England, of enslavers) and had little to say about African Americans at all. Eventually, it came to celebrate the famous saying by the Puritan minister John Winthrop that the nation would be like "a city on a hill."[8] The classic American story taught to children was one of wholesale goodness and an American exceptionalism that saw the United States not only as uniquely democratic but as patently the greatest country in the world and of all time.

One twentieth-century textbook in this lineage is *The Growth of the American Republic,* first published in 1930 by Samuel Eliot Morison and Henry Steele Commager and revised and used into the 1980s. Importantly, the book was not silent about slavery and African Americans, as some were; the inclusion of these topics was in many ways a liberal, even progressive move. Its presentation, however, was a telling product of its time. In its earlier editions, it said the following about American slavery (this is from the 1950 edition):

> As for Sambo, whose wrongs moved the abolitionists to wrath and tears, there is some reason to believe that he suffered less than any other class in the South from its "peculiar institution." The majority of slaves were adequately fed, well cared for, and apparently happy. Competent observers reported that they performed less labor than the hired man of the Northern states. . . . Although brought to America by force, the incurably optimistic Negro soon became attached to the country, and devoted to his "white folks." . . . [T]rained obedience kept most slaves faithful throughout the Civil War. . . . There was no physical repulsion from color in the South. White children were suckled by black mammies, and played promiscuously with the pickaninnies. . . . *[T]here was much to be said for slavery as a transitional status between barbarism and civilization.* The Negro learned his

master's language, received his religion, and accepted his moral standards. In return he contributed much besides his labor—music and humor for instance—to American civilization.[9]

The typical enslaved person, they wrote, was "the average child-like, improvident, humorous, prevaricating, and superstitious Negro," one similar to "Tom Sawyer's devoted Jim."[10] But Commager and Morison clearly presumed enslaved persons were learning, à la Gingrich, to have "a clear sense of what it meant to be an American," which if one were *African* American meant: thoroughly subservient to whites.

A history textbook for seventh-graders in Virginia first published in 1957, *Virginia: History, Government, Geography* likewise emphasized the happiness of enslaved people under their "owners" or "masters" (terms long used for enslavers) and glorified the Confederacy that sought to maintain slavery against the North. This and its sister textbooks for Virginia schoolchildren in other grades had been created in a process overseen by the Virginia History and Government Textbook Commission created in 1950 by the state's General Assembly, men who resented and resisted the civil rights initiatives advanced by President Harry Truman. "A feeling of strong affection existed between masters and slaves in a majority of Virginia homes," read one passage: "Life among the Negroes of Virginia in slavery times was generally happy. The Negroes went about in a cheerful manner making a living themselves and for those for whom they worked. They were not so unhappy as some Northerners thought they were." This sunny depiction was illustrated with scenes like that of a well-dressed African family departing a ship, with the smiling father shaking the hand of his kindly new white master. Claims like these upheld the Lost Cause narrative professing that enslaved people were perfectly satisfied living in slavery until meddling northern abolitionists came in to spoil it all, using "the United States mail to

Image of an enslaved family disembarking from a ship, from a seventh-grade Virginia history textbook first published in 1957 and in use until the late 1970s. (Photograph by Chris Preitauer)

CHAPTER 29

How the Negroes Lived under Slavery

SLAVE LAWS NOT STRICTLY ENFORCED

send their abusive literature into the South." Truly, the authors assured, Virginia "offered a better life for the Negroes than did Africa." Together, these books with their segregationist Confederate ideology were estimated to have reached more than a million students, Black as well as white, from 1957 to 1980, when the state finally adopted new textbooks.[11]

But the battles over teaching history were hardly over. At the national level, no educational leader was more influential from the 1980s into the early 1990s than Lynne Cheney, who chaired the National Endowment for the Humanities from 1986 to 1993 before founding a think tank for reforming higher education in a conservative direction. Cheney long focused on the problem, which she saw as enormous, with telling a politicized history to youth of all ages, including the nation's young children. In a famous 1994 op-ed in the *Wall Street Journal,* Cheney decried the new National History Standards—guidelines for K–12 teaching of U.S. history that were released that same year—as a shrine to the culture of conformity and victimization that had "unleashed the forces of political correctness." Among the problems she saw with the new standards was the deemphasis of important "white males" such as Robert E. Lee, John D. Rockefeller, Alexander Graham Bell, Thomas Edison, Jonas Salk, and the Wright Brothers and the overemphasis (as she saw it) of less influential African American leaders such as Harriet Tubman and left-leaning political organizations such as the Sierra Club and the National Organization for Women. The crux of her critique seemed to be that the new standards were overwhelmingly critical of white Americans, with too many mentions of depressing subjects like the long presence of the Ku Klux Klan and the feverish anti-Communist episode that came to be called McCarthyism. "The authors tend to save their unqualified admiration for people, places and events that are politically correct," Cheney complained. She concluded, "We are a better people than the National Standards indicate, and our children deserve to know it."[12]

Cheney's account got at the crux of what bothered this group of antirevisionist critics that included politicians and celebrity pundits and remained active at least a quarter century later: they wanted students' attention to be focused on the greatness of America and particularly of white America, including its prosperity and its benevolent values; and they wanted teachers and textbooks to teach that the nation's leaders—businessmen and politicians alike—have mostly acted from upright and selfless motives. This, she made clear, was "traditional history," not "the inclusive part" ostensibly demanded by "various political groups, such as African-American organizations and Native American groups." In Cheney's words, history-telling should offer a consistent "tone of affirmation" about America; it should teach the "positive cultural consequences" of wealth in developing culture and the "individual greatness that has flourished within our political institutions," and not, as the new standards urged, "ponder the paradox that the Constitution sidetracked the movement to abolish slavery that had taken rise in the revolutionary era." It should not be skewed, as she saw the new standards skewing, toward "'multiple perspectives' and on how the American Revolution did or did not serve the 'interests' of different groups."

From Cheney's perspective, an account that does not portray the United States in a primarily flattering light is essentially unpatriotic, really *anti*patriotic. Accounts that tell the stories of oppressed groups, in the words of one historian critical of this view (Peter Stearns), "tarnish the national image." What is instead desired is "a nice past, full of democracy and business success and opportunity, leading implicitly toward a nicer future[,] . . . [an] underlying tide of progress leading humankind or Americankind ever upward and onward." This is history-telling intended to be inspirational, something that "will infuse our young with proper values" and nationalistic pride.[13]

This was the sentiment expressed by Kansas senator Robert Dole when, in seeking the Republican presidential nomination in the mid-1990s, he condemned those he called "liberal academic elites" who taught history courses that presented some groups as victims and overemphasized negative events (like Cheney, his examples were "the scourge of McCarthyism and the rise of the Ku Klux Klan," movements that condemned multiple types of people but disproportionately targeted African Americans). Dole proclaimed that the main goal of teaching history ought to be instilling in students the unshakable belief that the United States is "the greatest country on the face of the Earth."[14] Condemning "political correctness" and "intellectual elites who seem embarrassed by America," Dole protested: "What we see as opportunity, they see as oppression. . . . Where we see a proud past, they see a legacy of shame. What we hold as moral truth, they call intolerance."[15] A World War II veteran, Dole condemned the Smithsonian

Institution exhibit that called dropping the atomic bomb "an act of American violence against Japanese culture" and concluded: "Maybe it's time the Embarrassed-About-America Crowd gets the message . . . : We're proud of our country. And we won't put up with our tax dollars being used to drag it down or sow doubt about the nobility of America in the minds of our children."[16]

Dole and Cheney's complaints were part of the antivictimism that emerged in the early 1990s and grew stronger with time. As Alyson Cole recounts in *The Cult of True Victimhood,* antivictimist critics have decried what they have seen as the manipulative claims of those foregrounding racial and gender-based oppression in U.S. history and seeking to remedy their long-term effects. In the process of developing their critiques of "victim politics," however, these critics have often assumed the mantle of True Victim: one who has been "ostracized, censored, and punished in other ways by political correctness, affirmative action, hate speech codes, and similar manifestations of injurious victim politics." Quite often those who have taken on this status of True Victim have been white men professing their moral uprightness and wholesale innocence from any wrong. Cole cites Gingrich as one of the architects of this "anti-victimist onslaught and . . . the drive to remasculinize America"; and she analyzes texts from the early 1990s written by Charles Sykes, Robert Hughes, Shelby Steele, Alan Dershowitz, and Dinesh D'Souza, among others, that accuse American scholars of being "obsessed with ferreting out real and imaginary past wrongs along lines of gender, sexuality, race, ethnicity, and class."[17]

An exceptionally sour depiction of the supposed degradations of political correctness comes from George Will, who has written quite a few of these; most are variations on the following, one of his earlier rebukes of the university's "politicized profs" who say: "America is oppressive, imposing subservience on victim groups.

The culture is permeated with racism, sexism, heterosexism, classism, so the universities' first task is 'consciousness-raising'" (a term I have not once heard in a university setting except when referring to second-wave feminism in the 1970s). According to Will: "The universities' imprimatur is bestowed on one view of American history, a political agenda. The status of victim is coveted for moral dignity and political power, so nerves are rubbed raw by the competitive cultivation of grievances. . . . Every academic activity must have an ameliorative dimension, reforming society and assuaging this or that group's grievance."[18] Dinesh D'Souza's book about the disease of political correctness spreading at universities, *Illiberal Education,* makes the same points and even titles its first chapter "The Victim's Revolution on Campus."[19]

Lingering on these critiques enables us to grasp the intensity of the resistance to academia's encouragement for expanding the actors visible in history and telling a story that is about more than American success and greatness. George Will accuses proponents of women's and African American history of competing for victim status, but the real subject of that column is his own victimization as someone whose preferred history might now be set alongside other histories. As Nash wryly concludes, in response to Gingrich, Cheney, Will, and their sympathizers: "If the rise of women's history or African American history or labor history has created a crisis, we must ask 'whose crisis'? The crisis, in fact, is in the minds of those whose monopolistic hold on the property of history has been shattered."[20] Those working to expand the canon were not trying to remove white men from history textbooks, not even heroic white men, not even conservative white men; they were trying to tell a fuller, fairer, and more truthful story about our nation's past and the many peoples who, in addition to those men, together made that history. It's *truthfulness* they were going for, not a political agenda or some power play against white men.

What do I mean by saying that that they wanted a fuller and fairer story, and in what way is that more truthful? A fuller and fairer account would be one that captures more people's stories and that is therefore more complete and more just to the multiplicity of experiences of the many different kinds of people who make up America. It is an account that includes people who have not previously been incorporated into the nation's mythology as anything more than marginal; and in trying to tell their stories, or listen to their voices through primary sources, we can encounter a broader, that is, *fuller* picture of America. This picture is *fairer* because it rectifies previous exclusions that were unjust, because in omitting actual people and their experiences it erased them and distorted the historical record. Surely this fuller, fairer story is not merely "politically correct" in some silly, frivolous way that's worthy of derision; like it or not, the fuller, fairer story is more truthful than other possible stories that exclude people from their narrative. It is more truthful because it engages in the project of asking how we know what the truth *is*—whether the history that we like and prefer is the history that really was; whether the history we've been told is all there is to say; and whether we can face the possibility that the history we were taught as kids was partial and even *un*truthful in certain ways that were not innocent—and our good fortune is the chance to face this fact and try to correct the illusions.

Moreover, this is an approach to a truthful story that teaches or reminds us that the truth is something to be actively sought and not necessarily ever completely found; that committing oneself to telling a truthful story requires constantly asking whether the account one is telling is the fullest and fairest that it can be. The historian will never reach perfect completion of the whole narrative, any narrative, but that is no excuse for willfully omitting people who were there for the action but whose experiences don't fit the narrative of what one wishes were true. Truthfulness here is a willful effort; it is a disciplined practice of seeking fuller and fairer accounts even when they hurt, of asking if and why our current accounts need revision (and what forces led to errors and exclusions) and making the necessary changes to help different parts of our history be heard, known, and understood.

Over a quarter century ago, the historians Joyce Appleby, Lynn Hunt, and Margaret Jacob advocated something like this in their book *Telling the Truth about History*. There they argued for a "democratic practice of history" in which "an ever-growing chorus of voices is heard," a practice that depended upon a revised concept of objectivity defined as "a commitment to honest investigation, open processes of research, and engaged public discussions of the meaning of historical facts." The highest goal of education remained: "the rigorous search for truth usable by all peoples." This should be an antidote to the false forms of patriotism that lie; as they wrote, "Nations keep their shape by molding their citizens' understanding of the past, causing its members to forget those events that do not accord with its righteous image while keeping alive those memories that do." Published in 1994, *Telling the Truth about History* was an intended contribution to the 1990s debates about history-telling and argued strongly against those traditionalists who had "created a new national bogey in the form of political correctness" and who claimed that historians like Appleby, Hunt, and Jacob were "filled with venomous hatred of Western civilization."[21]

Interestingly, the very next year Lynne Cheney titled one of her several books on this subject *Telling the Truth*, making clear that she believed it was the revisionists who were deceiving students with overly dismal portrayals of America. There she wrote that, "instead of being encouraged to search for a complicated truth, students are increasingly presented with oversimple versions of the American past that focus on the negative." She quoted from another observer that "Students . . . learn about racism as an American and European phenomenon only. Even though Islamic and African history are extensively covered in the curriculum . . . students learn only about the trans-Atlantic slave trade and nothing about the slave trade conducted by African kings or Arab traders for centuries preceding and following the trans-Atlantic slave trade."[22] Cheney's claim throughout is that she is arguing for students to learn a history of "complicated truths"—say, a story of Columbus and indigenous peoples as not a "good guys/bad guys" battle but an encounter in which there was brutality as well as heroism on both sides. Such an aim sounds virtuous, but one hunts in vain to find complicated truths in Cheney's own history books for children, such as *America: A Patriotic Primer* (2002), *Our Fifty States: A Family Adventure across America* (2006), and *We the People: The Story of Our Constitution* (2008), the latter of which covers slavery in a single breezy passage on the infamous Missouri Compromise and the decision to continue the slavery trade:

> To determine how many representatives a state would have, the convention decided to count three-fifths of the slaves. This compromise meant that the South would be part of the new government, but some delegates hated the bargain. Slavery was an evil institution, Gouverneur Morris raged, "the curse of heaven on the states where it prevailed." Such words would ring out in the State House again when the delegates debated a ban on bringing more slaves into the country. The convention decided that there could be no ban for twenty years. The delegates moved on to other decisions . . . George Washington went fishing.[23]

The meaning is unclear: are readers to side with Morris in see-ing slavery as an evil curse, or agree with the compromise that rendered enslaved people subhuman? In this instance, at least, children must come to their own conclusion as the story quickly marches on into American greatness.

This leave-it-to-the-reader tack may seem like the objectivity that many argue scholarship demands, or more likely the sim-plicity that a kids' book requires—certainly, children's books by their nature are simplifications. But the tone contrasts sharply with Cheney's recurrent celebratory exclamations like: "For cit-izens of our country, living on a vast and bountiful continent, it seemed a new age was dawning. A free and independent America would surely prosper and become a great and mighty nation."[24] One rationale for such lighthearted history-telling is familiar to any parent: the worry that telling children terrible truths could mar their hopeful idealism and cause despair or shock that people in their own country, even their own ancestors, could have done dreadful things. The institution of slavery stands so squarely against the doctrines of equality and inalienable rights that framed the nation's identity that it can seem too irreconcil-able a contradiction—an impossible stain to worry children about. Notably, African Americans never appear again in *We the People:* Like the historians of old described by Appleby, Hunt, and Jacob, it was as if Cheney took a virtual "vow of silence," knowing that the brutal segregation apparatus that succeeded slavery gave the lie to America's purportedly deepest ideals and so was "an incubus better denied than confronted."[25]

In the end, Cheney's allegedly "complicated truth" sounds less like a clear-eyed recounting of history's thorny problems and the morally questionable accommodations made by human beings past and present, than a reassuring cover-up message about white American goodness and innocence writ broadly. Cheney does not come right out and say this so bluntly in her writing; she doesn't have to. When it comes to race, whiteness is "a category of identity that is most useful when its very existence is denied," the Georgetown University scholar Michael Eric Dyson writes. "That's its twisted genius."[26]

A common strategy for deflecting these matters is to dismiss whites' attention to race and racism as "white guilt" and to object that it isn't necessary. On his radio show, Rush Limbaugh's recurring ruminations on slavery make this especially clear, such as this one:

> You know folks, it's time for all this white guilt to end. . . .
> [A] little history lesson for you. If any race of people should not
> have guilt about slavery, it's Caucasians. The white race has
> probably had fewer slaves and for a briefer period of time than
> any other in the history of the world. . . . [N]o other race has ever
> fought a war for the purpose of ending slavery, which we did.
> Nearly 600,000 people killed in the Civil War. It's preposterous
> that Caucasians are blamed for slavery when they've done more
> to end it than any other race, and within the bounds of the Con-
> stitution to boot. And yet white guilt is still one of the dominating
> factors in American politics. It's exploited, it's played upon, it is
> promoted, used, and it's unnecessary.[27]

As the journalist Jonathan Chait, citing this and other recordings, writes, "The grotesque unfairness, that white Americans are blamed for slavery when they should be credited for their relative lack of slavery, galls Limbaugh continuously."[28] One searches fruitlessly, though, to find a narrative accounting of American slavery's actual history (even a whitewashed version) anywhere in Limbaugh's body of work, or Cheney's. He's going for offense and outrage—not truth. She's going for pride in the glory of Anglo-Saxon America.

James Baldwin made one of the most compelling rejoinders to

these defenses against white guilt. In a 1964 essay titled "Words of a Native Son," he wrote:

> I'm not interested in anybody's guilt. Guilt is a luxury that we can no longer afford. I know you didn't do it, and I didn't do it either, but I am responsible for it because I am a man and a citizen of this country and you are responsible for it, too, for the very same reason: As long as my children face the future they face, and come to the ruin that they come to, your children are very greatly in danger, too. They are endangered above all by the moral apathy which pretends it isn't happening. This does something terrible to us.[29]

The pretense promoted by Limbaugh that liberals want white people to feel guilty about slavery, rather than work for justice in the present, feels like a convenient distraction, a way to rag on those fighting to excavate structural racism (perhaps intimidate them into silence) and remain comfortably in the status quo. In Baldwin's words from *The Fire Next Time,* white people asserting their innocence are "trapped in a history which they do not understand; and until they understand it, they cannot be released from it. They have had to believe for many years, and for innumerable reasons, that black men are inferior to white men. Many of them, indeed, know better, but, as you will discover, people find it very difficult to act on what they know."[30]

Limbaugh's reaction against "white guilt" is a clear example of these patterns, of what DiAngelo popularly terms "white fragility," in which "even a minimum amount of racial stress" feels excruciating and triggers belligerent denial to restore "white racial equilibrium" and enable white people to ignore their own role in upholding racism and keep doing what they're doing.[31] For Limbaugh, Cheney, Will, and Gingrich, the years prior to our

James Baldwin walking in New York, 1963. (AP Photo/Dave Pickoff)

own—really, prior to about 1965—were the American good old days, the time before lefty multiculturalists took over academia and culture. But scholars of race and racism have shown over and over again that this "good old days" reminiscing, the claim that the past was markedly better than the present, is a quintessential attribute of white supremacist ideology: it creates a gauzy, sentimentalized past that is at heart a lie, really a whole set of interconnected lies whose "most pernicious effect when it comes to our history," Eddie Glaude contends, "is to malform events to fit the story whenever America's innocence is threatened by reality." That lie is felt to be necessary because it is "the mechanism that allows, and has always allowed, America to avoid facing the truth about its unjust treatment of black people and how it deforms the soul of the country."[32] White people tell the story of pure American greatness and progress, and it boosts what DiAngelo calls "a deeply internalized sense of superiority and entitlement" along with a perception that "any advancement for people of color is an encroachment on this entitlement."[33] As the writers of *Telling the*

Truth about History put it in 1994, ten generations of white Americans suppressed from their memories and textbooks clear evidence of Black life in the antebellum South and thereby "shaped memory to the psychological needs of a white citizenry deeply conflicted by its persistent racial hostility." Or, in Fanon's famous portrayal of global colonialism: "The misfortune of the man of color is having been enslaved. The misfortune and inhumanity of the white man are having killed man somewhere. And still today they are organizing this dehumanization rationally."[34]

Truthfulness. The burden of speaking truthfully about American slavery and its legacies has often been carried overwhelmingly by African Americans. African American scholars have been the primary detectives to uncover and illuminate miles upon miles of archival sources that tell us who and what forces shaped the nation's slavery-drenched past and continue to shape our present. As a work of historical scholarship, W. E. B. Du Bois's classic study *Black Reconstruction in America, 1860–1880* (1935) is a milestone in this tradition, a "revisionist masterpiece," in the words of his biographer; it is also significant for its scathing critique of American history-telling on the part of whites seeking to prove their prior assumptions of Black inferiority. In the final chapter, "The Propaganda of History," Du Bois excoriated historical authors for teaching students that slavery was constitutional, that the abolitionists were bad, and "that Negroes were the only people to achieve emancipation with no effort on their part":

> One is astonished in the study of history at the recurrence of
> the idea that evil must be forgotten, distorted, skimmed over. . . .
> We must forget that George Washington was a slave owner, or
> that Thomas Jefferson had mulatto children, or that Alexander

W. E. B. Du Bois at his desk in his home office, New York, 1958. (David Attie/Michael Ochs Archives/Getty Images)

Hamilton had Negro blood, and simply remember the things we regard as creditable and inspiring. The difficulty, of course, with this philosophy is that history loses its value as an incentive and example; it paints perfect men and noble nations, but it does not tell the truth.

As Du Bois analyzed in detail, histories of the Civil War and Reconstruction were "written in the main by those who were convinced before they began to write that the Negro was incapable of government, or of becoming a constituent part of a civilized state." They were "cajoling and flattering the South" in allowing its white innocence narrative to flourish; but this completely distorted the facts and erased the history of African Americans. It led Americans to "embrace and worship the color bar as social salvation" and to "range mankind in ranks of mutual hatred and contempt, at the summons of a cheap and false myth."[35]

Du Bois described himself as "literally aghast at what American historians have done to this field," for "in propaganda against the Negro since emancipation in this land, we face one of the most stupendous efforts the world ever saw to discredit human beings, an effort involving universities, history, science, social life and religion." He called for historians to "regard the truth as more important than the defense of the white race" and to teach their students likewise, but he had little hope of this happening; his furious summary of the fruits of white-innocence/Black-subordination education in his day came at the very end of the book, a shattering rebuke: "Immediately in Africa, a black back runs red with the blood of the lash; in India, a brown girl is raped; in China, a coolie starves; in Alabama, seven darkies are more than lynched; while in London, the white limbs of a prostitute are hung with jewels and silk. Flames of jealous murder sweep the earth, while brains of little children smear the hills." White innocence is murderous, Du Bois insists; and while the truth may hurt, it also helps repair the damage done by lies: "Nations reel and stagger on their way; they make hideous mistakes; they commit frightful wrongs; they do great and beautiful things. And shall we not best guide humanity by telling the truth about all this, so far as the truth is ascertainable?"[36]

Since Du Bois wrote those words in 1935, decades of painstaking, pathbreaking scholarship have made an enormous impact on the way children and adolescents in many American schools learn about U.S. history. But plenty of school systems still resist including "too much" about slavery and racism in their history textbooks and literature classes. Progress has been very uneven, to say the least. In his important book *Lies My Teacher Told Me: Everything Your American History Textbook Got Wrong,* the sociologist and historian James Loewen wryly puts it this way (referring to whites): "Americans seem perpetually startled at slavery," and even the newer textbooks that cover slavery in somewhat greater detail make it out to be "an unfortunate but minor blemish" in an overall optimistic narrative of U.S. history.[37]

For instance, research conducted in 2017 by the nonprofit Southern Poverty Law Center surveyed American high school seniors, social studies teachers in all grades, fifteen state content standards, and ten widely taught U.S. history textbooks. Researchers discovered the following, documented in their published report *Teaching Hard History: American Slavery:*

- Only 8 percent of high school seniors knew slavery was the central cause of the Civil War.
- Two-thirds (68 percent) did not know that slavery ended formally because of a constitutional amendment.
- Fewer than one in four students correctly identified the constitutional provisions that advantaged owners of enslaved people.
- Although more than 90 percent of teachers claimed to feel "comfortable" discussing slavery with students, survey results showed that they feel "profound unease" around it.
- Of the fifteen sets of state standards that were analyzed, according to the report, "none addresses how the ideology of white supremacy rose to justify the institution of slavery; most fail to lay out meaningful requirements for learning about slavery, about the lives of millions of enslaved people, or about how their labor was essential to the American economy."

Researchers concluded, among other things, that teachers tend to "present the good news before the bad" and, indeed, the good news *in lieu of* the bad—learning about the Underground Railroad, Frederick Douglass and white abolitionists, the Emancipation Proclamation, or various "feel-good" stories but not about the slavery system itself or its legacies in racist structures whose effects persist into, and thoroughly permeate, our own time. And this was in 2017, decades after the historian George Unwin's observation that British historians included slavery only in its abolition.[38]

In a point that is particularly well worded, the report's writers note: "We tend to subscribe to a progressive view of American history that can acknowledge flaws only to the extent that they have been addressed and solved. Our vision of growing ever 'more perfect' stands in the way of our need to face the continuing legacy of the past."[39] Teachers and textbooks tend to minimize slavery in any number of ways: they suggest that it was only a southern institution, not one that was present throughout all the colonies and all the states at the time of the signing of the Declaration of Independence and beyond. They typically don't connect slavery to the ideology of white supremacy created to justify it that remains alive and well in this country still, notably illustrated by events such as the 2017 Unite the Right rally in Charlottesville, Virginia, which brought together neo-Nazis and other white supremacist groups; or the increasing number of mass shootings openly motivated by the white power movement.[40]

Indeed, teachers and textbooks might note that from 1619, the year the first enslaved Africans were imported into Jamestown, until 1865, when the Thirteenth Amendment abolished slavery, equals 246 years of legal bondage; but this can feel like ancient history to those who feel themselves to be untouched by it. Teachers and textbooks typically don't connect slavery to the present at all, as a crucial context for understanding the controversy over Confederate memorials in cities and towns not just in the South but across the whole country and even beyond. Hundreds of Confederate statues were erected across the United States in the decades following the Civil War. More than 150 years after the war ended, these still stood in public places in thirty-one states: from Alabama to Alaska to California (where until recently there were at least eight Confederate memorials, including a "Johnny Rebel" mascot at an Anaheim high school and a Jeff Davis Peak, as well as a Robert E. Lee giant sequoia in a park run by the National Park Service), Georgia to Hawaii (where a plaque in the

National Memorial Cemetery of the Pacific honored Hawaiians who fought in the Civil War, including for the Confederacy), Idaho and other states in the "Wild West," New Jersey and New York, and Virginia—which has hosted more Confederate monuments than any other state. Such statues went beyond U.S. borders and could be found even in Brazil, and even Canada. According to the Southern Poverty Law Center's data and reporting in *Teaching Hard History,* it is, in fact, quite likely that large numbers of Americans did not learn anything about the history of Confederate monuments in school; and so those who deny that these monuments are celebrations of slavery and the ideology of white supremacy may be genuinely ignorant of their history.

In his magisterial book *The Half Has Never Been Told: Slavery and the Making of American Capitalism* (2014), the historian Edward E. Baptist argues forcefully, and with meticulously gathered empirical data for support, that the great driver of the Industrial Revolution in America, and hence the greatest source of the nation's subsequent long prosperity, was the brutally violent slavery system that tore children from their mothers' arms, split husbands from wives, and permanently scarred and killed more Black bodies than will ever receive a full count. "The idea that the commodification and suffering and forced labor of African Americans is what made the United States powerful and rich is not an idea that people necessarily are happy to hear," writes Baptist. "Yet it is the truth." What slavery's survivors endured was "a slavery that didn't fit the comfortable boxes into which other Americans have been trying to fit it ever since it ended."[41] As Baptist recounts, between the 1790s and the 1860s, slavery traders and enslavers moved a million people from older slavery states to ones newly formed and badly in need of economic development. There was virtually no cotton trade in the United States in 1790; by 1860, enslaved persons were producing nearly two billion pounds of it per year. Baptist tells a sweeping story that extends far beyond the slavery South and politicians who supported the system to "Connecticut factories, London banks, opium addicts in China, and consumers in East Africa. . . . Changes that reshaped the entire world began on the auction block where enslaved migrants stood or in the frontier cotton fields where they toiled."[42]

In another innovative history of the American slavery system, *Accounting for Slavery: Masters and Management,* Caitlin Rosenthal shows how plantation owners distanced themselves from the harsh realities of slavery: "Running a slave plantation involved lots of data carefully entered into paper spreadsheets and reports. . . . From the comfort of counting rooms, plantation owners could review this data without having to think too hard about the people it represented." Owners of the enslaved carefully measured the cotton output of their plantations and masked the births and deaths of enslaved people with "chilling economic shorthand" that spoke vaguely of the "'increase' and 'decrease' of laborers." Rosenthal summarizes:

> When you understand the context of these records—high
> mortality, punishing slave labor, racialized violence—the records
> are horrifying. . . . Even as the data illuminated productivity, it
> obscured other aspects of plantation life. . . . Plantation own-
> ers . . . could manage assets and maximize value without con-
> sidering the horrifying violence of plantation life. They could
> calculate how to accelerate production without considering the
> exploitative conditions that made this speedup possible. Or pon-
> der how to increase efficiency without dwelling on the synergies
> between their calculations and the overseer's whip.[43]

We're talking about millions upon millions of enslaved persons, over 246 years. In Baptist's words, "slavery's expansion shaped every crucial aspect of the economy and politics of the new nation."[44]

Even the very fact that the Civil War was about slavery has been a fact hotly denied and buried (as witnessed by the figure cited above that only 8 percent of students recognized slavery as the cause). James Loewen has written about this in *Lies My Teacher Told Me,* showing that most Americans have typically believed that secession from the Union by the southern states was about states' rights, not slavery; in fact, he points out, South Carolina's very secession decree excoriated the free states that wanted to exercise states' rights by refusing to capture freedom seekers escaping into their territories or to return them to their enslavers. (Though bound by the federal Fugitive Slave Act, many found ways around it.) "Carolinians," he continues, "also contested the rights of residents of other states even to *think* differently about their peculiar institution, giving as another reason for secession that Northerners 'have denounced as sinful the institution of slavery.'" The "abiding purpose of secession," Loewen makes clear, was the protection of slavery; to insist that it was states' rights is "Southern apologetics" developed to absolve the South from the truth. It is revealing that this demonstrable reality has been so hidden in U.S. textbooks; but "a topic that is mystified or distorted in our history, like secession, usually signifies a continuing injustice in the present, like racism."[45]

Are white people living today to blame for the institution of slavery? Was this their (our) fault? Of course not. Have white people benefited, and still continue to benefit, from the labor of enslaved human beings? Indubitably yes, in a vast array of ways. The continued willful ignorance of the twenty-five decades of slavery in America and its perpetual aftermath has done untold damage to white people's own integrity, capacity for empathy, and attunement to full equality and justice. Even as late as February 2019, in an Ashburn, Virginia, elementary school, an activity supposedly crafted to celebrate Black History Month taught third-, fourth-, and fifth-graders (white and Black) about the Underground Railroad by having them play a game in which they were runaway enslaved persons—seeming to make light of the terrors faced by real people seeking freedom from enslavement (after receiving complaints and media attention, the school apologized).[46] Such an incident seems in keeping with recent children's books that extol the happy conditions of enslaved children and their enslaved parents: these include *A Fine Dessert,* published by an imprint of Random House and nominated for several book prizes, including a Caldecott award; and *A Birthday Cake for George Washington,* which reaped an outcry after Scholastic published it in 2016 and was soon recalled. Both books featured children learning from their parents how to cook for and serve their benevolent white masters.[47] Such incidents that trivialize or even extol the happy conditions of slavery only extend the racial ignorance into future generations.

The Jamaican philosopher Charles Mills has written compellingly about the phenomenon he calls "white ignorance," which he views as a "particularly pervasive . . . form of ignorance . . . linked to white supremacy." He opens his analysis:

> White ignorance . . .
> It's a big subject. How much time do you have?
> It's not enough. . . .
> Imagine an ignorance that resists.
> Imagine an ignorance that fights back.
> Imagine an ignorance militant, aggressive, not to be intimidated, an ignorance that is active, dynamic, that refuses to go quietly—not at all confined to the illiterate and uneducated but propagated at the highest levels of the land, indeed presenting itself unblushingly as knowledge.[48]

This is the sort of ignorance that could lead a U.S. president to say, as one did in 2017: "People don't realize, you know, the Civil War . . . When you think about it, why? People don't ask that question, but why was there the Civil War? Why could that one not have been worked out?" It's the sort manifested in, and perpetuated by, the televised August 2019 remark by Fox News host Tucker Carlson—in the wake of mass shootings in El Paso, Texas, and Dayton, Ohio, that killed dozens of people—that called warnings of rising white supremacy "a hoax" and "conspiracy theory used to divide the country."[49] It drove the ideology of the January 6 Capitol insurrection *and* the astonished reaction to it. Militant ignorance is alive and well in white America.

Ignorance—the state of being unaware or uninformed about something—begets ignorance. It also cultivates vulnerability to lies and propaganda, to easy assurances that persons or institutions one wants to believe in are perfectly innocent, benevolent forces in the world whereas those one dislikes are worthy of mistrust, disapproval, and even banishment. We are all ignorant of many more things than we ordinarily recognize or reckon with, and our ignorance can make us susceptible to "fake news" that casts shadows on things that feel foreign to us. Such ignorance has been one of the roots of nativism throughout our country's history, and it has nourished both fear and hatred of strangers in countless other geographical and cultural settings as well.

This ignorance-born fear may be a normal part of the animal and human condition, but it has proven to be dangerously exploitable in our current media-fractured age, where "fake news" can transform from a murmur to an earsplitting uproar almost instantaneously, and where bald-faced lying thrives in presidential pronouncements, among other places. And I'm afraid that as a nation we—that is, an overwhelming majority of Americans across various political and ideological spectrums—have become precariously habituated and accustomed to public lying as just a normal part of civic life. We have come to expect politicians to lie to us; we may not like it, or too much of it around issues we care about individually, but we've become desensitized to political lies much of the time. Demanding honesty from our leaders feels almost childishly gullible; "of course they lie, or they'd get voted out of office," we say. Lying erodes trust, there's no question about that, and yet it seems more and more that many Americans tolerate the lies of their favorite political leaders if the lies represent something that we wish were true or that we want others to believe. Americans don't just *tolerate* these lies, in fact; many help spread them.

Perhaps this is too sweeping a depiction of this state of affairs; possibly I've oversimplified. Plenty of people despair of the prevalence of lying in various sectors of public life, whether by politicos fabricating heroic autobiographies, celebrities whitewashing nasty misbehavior, or church officials systematically covering up criminal sexual abuse. Many people would likely welcome a higher standard of truth-telling for those who hold power over our institutions, our economic well-being, and the welfare of the nation's children. A stronger commitment to addressing genuinely complicated truths in the telling of our nation's history is a critical factor as well.

In talking about a renewal in our valuations of truthfulness, I'm not speaking of private life. In fact, political and religious leaders all too often talk about truth-telling as if it were only a private moral value: teach children not to lie to their parents, chastise husbands who lie to their wives about adulterous affairs, condemn lying in your domestic and interpersonal life. Those are important issues, but intimate, interpersonal lying is not the subject here. It is, rather, lies that get told for political gain, lies that are conveyed about the nation and its history. Sometimes these are active lies of commission—direct and intentional falsehoods—and sometimes they are passive lies of omission—factual truths left untold, intentionally or ignorantly, or maybe reliance on what can appropriately be named propaganda.

During his presidency in the 1980s, Ronald Reagan—nicknamed "The Great Communicator" for his fluent speechmaking—frequently paraphrased John Winthrop to inspire in his listeners a vision of America as the "shining city upon a hill." In his farewell speech to the nation in January 1989, as he was headed out after eight years in the White House, Reagan spoke with his usual eloquence to issue a final warning to Americans about the need to cultivate an "informed patriotism," and his rendering of recent American history was telling. He started by noting that "one of the things I'm proudest of [from] the past eight years" was "the resurgence of national pride that I called the new patriotism." But he worried that this national pride was frail and vulnerable to cynicism. He urged adults to consider how they taught children about America so as to cultivate "an informed patriotism . . . grounded in thoughtfulness and knowledge," as Reagan insisted had been done in the "different America"—a more patriotic one, it seemed—of his own childhood:

> We were taught, very directly, what it means to be an American. And we absorbed, almost in the air, a love of country and an appreciation of its institutions. If you didn't get these things from your family you got them from the neighborhood, from the father down the street who fought in Korea or the family who lost someone at Anzio. Or you could get a sense of patriotism from school. And if all else failed you could get a sense of patriotism from the popular culture. The movies celebrated democratic values and implicitly reinforced the idea that America was special. TV was like that, too, through the mid-sixties.

Unfortunately, Reagan continued, much was now changed: popular culture no longer cultivated patriotism, and "parents aren't sure that an unambivalent appreciation of America is the right thing to teach modern children."

It was crucial, warned the president, to get across the message "that America is freedom—freedom of speech, freedom of religion, freedom of enterprise." Freedom could not survive without nurture and protection; it was "special and rare . . . fragile." Children needed to gain inspiration by learning about the Pilgrims, the soldiers of World War II, and other heroes of American history. Warning of "an eradication of the American memory that could result, ultimately, in an erosion of the American spirit," Reagan urged the nation to start with the basics: "more attention to American history and a greater emphasis on civic ritual."[50]

"More attention to history" is an excellent proposal, without doubt. But Reagan's idea of what that meant—"an unambivalent appreciation of America"—came very close to Lynne Cheney's version—all greatness, no mistakes. Freedom is "fragile" and needs protection, enacted by pure patriotic celebration: we protect freedom purely by celebrating it, in other words—not talking about how some Americans have been freer than others, or brutally prevented others from enjoying any freedom whatsoever. Notably, it was Reagan who (in 1988) signed the congressional resolution apologizing for the internment of the Japanese during World War II; that was an important example of acknowledging a grave wrong committed by American leaders against an ethnic minority. But there was no apology to African Americans for 246 years of slavery and decades more of Jim Crow racism and segregation.

Contrast Reagan's "informed patriotism" of pure American greatness to the view expressed by the equally eloquent Barack Obama in his 2015 speech commemorating the fiftieth anniversary of "Bloody Sunday" in Selma, Alabama. There he talked about patriotism as an ongoing project of self-criticism and remaking:

"What greater expression of faith in the American experiment than this; what greater form of patriotism is there; than the belief that America is not yet finished, that we are strong enough to be self-critical, that each successive generation can look upon our imperfections and decide that it is in our power to remake this nation to more closely align with our highest ideals?" True patriotism, he continued, is an idea long held by those Americans who have believed that "America is a constant work in progress" and that "loving this country requires more than singing its praises or avoiding uncomfortable truths. It requires the occasional disruption, the willingness to speak out for what's right and shake up the status quo. That's America!"[51]

Obama went on to extol the indisputable progress that has occurred in this country in terms of the rights of African Americans, women, LGBTQ Americans, and more. Denying such progress was both factually and ethically wrong; but, he argued, the greater error was the suggestion that racism was a problem fully solved and that those who pointed out persistent discrimination were false victims and opportunists. The country's racist past still haunted the present, and the only way to remedy racism was "facing up to the truth": "That's what it means to love America. That's what it means to believe in America. That's what it means when we say America is exceptional." America was "not stock photos or airbrushed history or feeble attempts to define some of us as more American as others." There was no reason for Americans to pine for some idealized past nor to fear the future, for all would be well. Quoting Whitman, Obama assured his listeners that "America is not some fragile thing" but "large . . . containing multitudes."[52]

In many respects, these two calls to American pride in our past, by President Reagan in 1989 and President Obama twenty-six years later, are quite similar: *don't give up on our great country* is the core message of both speeches. Moreover, Obama's insistence that the United States is "exceptional" is an important reminder that American exceptionalism can and does flourish on the left as well as on the right. But the presidents' contrasting usages of "fragile" encapsulates the deep difference in how they believe American pride and patriotism will best be nurtured: In Reagan's mind, freedom itself is fragile and needs parents to instill "an unambivalent appreciation of America" in their children in order to endure. For Obama, "America is not some fragile thing" that shrivels and dies under critical scrutiny; telling its "true" story (Obama invoked notions of "true" four times in his speech) demands not so much ambivalence as a practice of critical truthfulness, beginning with an understanding that the ugly parts be fully recognized and grappled with (not rapidly passed over) along with the things that make the nation beautiful and can be celebrated. Seeing the full picture instead of some airbrushed version of it and admitting our faults would help citizens continue to believe in the nation's "sacred promise": "That's what it means to love America."

The point isn't to sort out what sort of patriotism is best, or to argue whether or not patriotism is a good thing at all. Obama may have been as naïve in his optimistic evaluation of American progress as Reagan was in his critique of honest engagement with the past, and presidential speeches are hardly impartial sites for learning anything true. The point of contrasting these speeches is to think about what it means to talk truthfully about the uglier aspects of American history in the hope of learning from them, versus what it means to stow the unpleasant parts silently away in the belief that they will only bring us down.

Remembering slavery is critical for Americans not merely for the sake of understanding long-ago history. Slavery's legacies have endured into our own time: The structural racism that white enslavement of Black people built in America lived on throughout Reconstruction and the Jim Crow South, upholding obstacles to African Americans trying to work their way up out of the poverty many were left in after emancipation. White supremacy made racial segregation an almost impenetrable force to dismantle until the Supreme Court's 1954 decision in *Brown v. Board of Education*. And even then, white Americans remained adept at resisting desegregation both directly and indirectly, sometimes violently: for example, in 1956, Texas segregationists brandished guns in the streets of Mansfield and set fire to an African American effigy in an effort to keep Black students out of the local high school; the next year, white mobs screamed and jeered at the nine African American teens who enrolled at Little Rock Central High School; and Black students attempting to attend southern universities such as the University of Alabama, the University of Mississippi, and the University of Georgia were greeted with riots. More than a decade after the court's decision, the U.S. Commission on Civil Rights noted, "Violence against Negroes continues to be a deterrent to school desegregation."[53] Over and over, white residents found loopholes to prevent the growth of racially diverse neighborhoods and public school districts, fleeing racially mixed cities into rapidly expanding rings of suburbs that grew whiter the farther they extended, and making sure tax dollars from affluent towns paid for goods and services only there rather than benefiting needier towns and school systems outside their borders.[54]

The racist views of white presidents and lawmakers did not only affect Black Americans during the time of Thomas Jefferson and other administrations prior to emancipation. These have carried through the years since. Richard Nixon, a president whose racism was particularly well documented on White House tapes, promoted both domestic and foreign policies shaped by white supremacy. He believed Blacks were inferior to whites, saying once to Daniel Patrick Moynihan: "I'm not saying that blacks cannot govern; I am saying they have a hell of a time. Now, that must demonstrate something." Reagan—caught on tape complaining to Nixon about African delegates to the United Nations as "those monkeys from those African countries—damn them, they're still uncomfortable wearing shoes!"—later very successfully wielded the racist trope of the lazy and promiscuous "welfare queen" to fire up emotions against poor Black women and swing American attitudes in the direction of dismantling social welfare programs.[55] The dehumanization of Black people that showed in these men's speech—Nixon chortled after Reagan's "monkeys" comment and repeated it to several other White House officials, calling the African leaders "cannibals" in the process—also manifested in their policy preferences.

Consider: the Reagan administration's aggressive taxation plan that slashed rates for corporations and the wealthiest 1 percent of Americans—for instance, Reagan reduced the top marginal tax rates from 70 percent to 28 percent, enabling the net worth of the Forbes "400 Richest Americans" to triple from 1978 to 1990—had a dramatic impact on economic inequality. "Under Reagan's tax policies," writes Ian Haney López, "the process of transferring wealth from the poor and the middle class to the rich and especially to the super-rich began with a vengeance," with enormous consequences for Blacks. African Americans were also affected by the Reagan administration's opposition to affirmative action and to court-ordered school desegregation, a hostility so forceful that the former assistant attorney general for the Civil Rights Division in the Carter administration lamented, "What they seek is no less than a relitigation of Brown v. Board of Education." The GOP platform plank on affirmative action during Reagan's 1984 reelection campaign directly opposed affirmative action by noting, "Quotas are the most insidious form of discrimination: reverse discrimination against the innocent." As Haney López observes: "The document said nothing about race directly, but obviously 'the innocent' meant innocent whites. Attacking affirmative action provided a way for the GOP to constantly force race—and the party's defense of white interests—into the national conversation."[56] Clearly, it also served to reinforce the comforting myth of white innocence and victimization.

Some of the deeply entwined catastrophic social problems of our time—urban poverty, the violent parastate created by the illegal drug economy, and mass incarceration—have their roots in, and are relentlessly nourished by, structural racism. Danielle Allen writes about this in *Cuz*, her heartbreaking memoir about a young cousin's incarceration and violent death, writing of how so many of us "turn a blind eye" to our own participation in the oppressive systems that lead to the conditions so painfully evident in his short life and the millions more who have been lost to prison, gang wars, and drugs: "We are like nineteenth-century Englishmen and -women who sweetened their tea with sugar made by slaves."[57] We blithely consume things made possible by the servitude of others. A direct legacy of slavery and its aftermath is the enormous wealth gap between Black and white Americans: according to a 2020 study based on the Survey of Consumer Finances (2004–16) directed by sociologists at Duke and Northwestern, Black households with children had only one cent for every dollar owned by white households with children. In another study of this data going back to 1949, a group of German economists starkly conclude, "No progress has been made in reducing income and wealth inequalities between black and white households over the past 70 years." As Nikole Hannah-Jones puts it bluntly, "Slavery and the 100-year period of racial apartheid and racial terrorism known as Jim Crow were, above all else, systems of economic exploitation."[58]

Attentiveness to the historical reality that these disastrous social and economic conditions are the legacy of slavery is difficult for some people, because it leads directly into territory that many whites find unpleasant to think about: the question of reparations. Are the descendants of enslaved persons owed some form of financial compensation for the decades of discrimination and economic inequity they have unfairly endured? If so, how will that be calculated? What will the total sum be? Where will that money come from? If African Americans are to receive reparations, what about Native Americans whose land was taken from them by white settlers? And on and on.

Many white leaders have staunchly resisted talk of reparations. Responding to the subject of reparations in June 2019, Senate Majority Leader Mitch McConnell (R-KY) said, "America should not be held liable for something that happened 150 years ago, since none of us currently alive are responsible." As Ta-Nehisi Coates pointed out at a subsequent congressional hearing on legislation about studying reparations, McConnell's words indicated "a strange theory of governance: that American accounts are somehow bound by the lifetimes of its generations." But pensions to the heirs of Civil War soldiers, Coates noted, were still being paid out well into the twenty-first century; treaties going back two hundred years were still honored; and Americans are taxed all the time for things for which they are not personally responsible, because it is for the larger collective good. Moreover, McConnell was alive (continued Coates) for countless horrors and plundering of African Americans in his own native state of Alabama, his adopted state of Kentucky, and many more. Coates, who has thought and written deeply about the subject of reparations to wide acclaim, showed how easy it is to poke holes in the ideological objections to reparations.[59] That may be moot for now, as a 2019 Gallup poll showed that 67 percent of Americans overall opposed the government making cash payments to descendants of the enslaved; while 73 percent of non-Hispanic Blacks were in favor, among non-Hispanic whites only 16 percent supported reparations.[60] Few white people want to risk giving up some of what they've got.

Like German reparations to Jewish victims of Nazis, American programs could go well beyond lump sum payments to individual people: scholarships, property investments, pensions, education programs, organizations that provide healthcare, community initiative for African Americans, and more.[61] There is, in fact, a great deal that can be done to remedy the racial imbalances and injustices that are the product of slavery's long legacy of white supremacist ideology and structural racism. Facing that legacy by learning the history and teaching it to children and other Americans is a necessary if insufficient step in that process. Refusing to do so is the surest way to breed among some in the next generation a righteous rage, and, among others, indifferent complicity.

Cultivating truthfulness about our nation's past and present—in all of its beauty and its ugliness, the suffering Americans have inflicted on people inside as well as far outside these borders and the care and nurture and protection we have offered one another and others in the world—this will not leave us hopeless. There is a great deal in America's history worth cherishing and preserving, even as there are other parts of our history for which we owe not simply apology but concrete attempts at restitution. Slavery and its legacies constitute one such part (the brutal treatment of Native Americans is another—and there are more). The way to create a more hopeful future is surely not to gloss over the past or seek to re-create a gullible form of patriotism that imagines our forefathers and -mothers to have been saints. Love of country need not be so different from love of family members whom one knows to be flawed, sometimes maddening, sometimes capable of really bad things for which they (and we) must make amends.

If facing the complicated history of the United States means not telling only the happy stories, as well as not telling only the awful stories (as many conservatives have accused liberals of doing), it means truthfully confronting our ancestors both for inspiration and in the hope that we may do better. The enslavement of Africans and their descendants for nearly a quarter of a millennium is one of the most urgent historical realities white Americans must confront. But slavery is not the only issue Americans have often had difficulty facing. Other topics provoke unease, to greater or lesser degrees. One of them is our nation's long conflict over immigration, to which I turn in the next chapter.

2

EMPATHY

*Aliens, Immigrants, and Strangers
in U.S. Policy*

Send her back! Send her back!
Send her back! Send her back! ...

—Trump rally attendees jeering Somali-born
U.S. Rep. Ilhan Omar, July 17, 2019

IN AN AMERICAN SUMMER filled with shocking events, one of
the most stunning occurred on a mid-July evening in 2019. At a
campaign rally for President Trump in Greenville, North Carolina, supporters loudly chanted, "Send her back!" after the
president condemned Minnesota representative Ilhan Omar, a
Somali-born naturalized U.S. citizen, for "looking down with contempt on the hard-working Americans" and for what he labeled
"vicious, anti-Semitic screeds."[1] The ensuing uproar was so severe
that the president claimed the next day that he "was not happy
with it" and that he had tried to stop the chanting by resuming
his speech "very quickly" after it started, a claim promptly dis-
proven by video evidence. Omar herself, in a *New York Times*

op-ed the following week, called Trump's rally "a defining moment in American history," prompting us to consider anew the grave urgency of the stakes at hand, "a fight for the soul of our nation."[2]

The anti-Omar rally chants, which came just after the president tweeted attacks against the Minnesota representative and three other freshman Democrats and women of color in the House of Representatives (Alexandria Ocasio-Cortez, Ayanna Pressley, and Rashida Tlaib)—"Why don't they go back and help fix the totally broken and crime infested places from which they came"—invoked her status as an immigrant for a reason.[3] Trump supporters' reaction unfolded amid months of controversy over U.S. immigration and asylum policies at the Mexico-U.S. border. The harshness of U.S. border policies, the horrific living conditions for those adults and children detained in filthy and freezing cages, and, above all, the casual indifference with which federal agencies appeared to have been separating migrant families without a plan for reuniting them spurred ferocious outrage among many (though by no means all) Americans. Critics of the government's techniques were met with censure from supporters that caricatured protesters' position as one supporting "open borders," and on flew the bombast, making little difference in the lives of those affected.

Perhaps Omar was right in calling this a "defining moment" in our history. But we have been in comparable moments before. Long disagreements over immigration policy—who to let in, how many, under what criteria, etc.—have characterized the United States throughout our history. American attitudes toward foreigners wanting to migrate here have vacillated across a remarkably wide range, and legal regulations of immigration have swung like a pendulum since the nineteenth century. Here, once again, it's important to know that history in at least rudimentary form, so as to better understand how our ideas of belonging and citizenship have been shaped over time.

Between 1880 and 1924, some twenty-five million people across many parts of the world left their homes, most of their possessions, friends, and many family members, and everything familiar to them for America, hoping to immigrate. Vast numbers of them were fleeing hunger; others sought refuge from prejudice and discrimination. Many trekked for days or weeks across Europe to get to a port city where they could board a ship. If they were wealthy, they could pay for decent staterooms for the journey that would take weeks. If they were not, they might find themselves in the vast open space on the ship's bottom, the cheapest quarters. Roughly twelve million of these people came through Ellis Island, sometimes up to six thousand a day going through the famous "Great Hall," where they had to undergo medical exams and legal interrogation about their reasons for coming to the United States and what kind of residents they would be. Most were concentrated from particular parts of Europe, but occasionally newcomers came from farther parts. As Edward Steiner, an Austrian Jewish immigrant, wrote in his vividly detailed 1906 book, *On the Trail of the Immigrant*: "Let no one believe that landing on the shores of 'The land of the free, and the home of the brave' is a pleasant experience; it is a hard, harsh fact, surrounded by the grinding machinery of the law, which sifts, picks, and chooses; admitting the fit and excluding the weak and helpless."[4]

Thousands failed the medical exam and landed in the hospital there that opened in 1902—twenty-two buildings on a separate part of Ellis Island that were built from the rock and dirt excavated from the construction of New York's subway system. Hundreds of babies were born in that hospital, not far from the unit for

Immigrants to the United States landing at Ellis Island, New York, ca. 1900. (The Print Collector/Alamy Stock Photo)

those perceived to be insane, not far from the surgical unit, not far from patients with cholera, diphtheria, polio, typhus, hookworm, measles, trachoma, and more. As Dr. Alfred Reed, a surgeon at Ellis Island, wrote in 1912, "There is a constant stream of fresh infection pouring in."[5] The hospital was intended to prevent that disease from making its way onshore and infecting the American populace, and health officials offered a very high level of care so as to cure the patients and protect the nation. Immigrant children who presented with symptoms might be taken away from their families, and because they did not share a language with their caregivers, many had no way of knowing what would happen to them or if they would ever see their parents again. Roughly 3,500 immigrants died in that hospital, many of them children. Tens of thousands more regained their health and became well enough to enter the United States. As the filmmaker Lorie Conway says, "The hospital was where America's conflicting beliefs about immigration collided—at once welcoming and threatening."[6]

Not all were warmly received. Most Americans today know that there were deep wells of anti-Irish and anti-Catholic sentiment in nineteenth-century America that persisted well into the twentieth century. Nativism, the open preference for white native-born Americans over immigrants, long exhibited itself in open prejudice against Irish Catholics, Asians, and Italians, among others. Anti-immigration cartoonists caricatured European and Asian foreigners as apelike idiots, thieves, and carriers of poverty and disease. They were illustrated overtaking the Democratic Party and stealing elections, drinking enormous quantities of rum, desecrating the Sabbath, taking away jobs from U.S. workers, and bringing Catholicism and other false religions and superstition into Protestant America. Whatever they were pictured doing, it was destroying the nation. All along, there were critics who believed U.S. immigration policy was far too lenient and needed tightening.

In 1882, the passage of the Chinese Exclusion Act became the first major piece of legislation to restrict immigration to the United States. It limited further immigration by the Chinese, who had come in significant numbers the previous decade and procured work on the railroads. Chinese immigration was completely suspended for ten years, and Chinese were declared ineligible for naturalization, that is, citizenship. Various amendments and renewals of that act sought to prevent Chinese immigration altogether, and in 1902 Chinese immigration was made permanently illegal. The Chinese already in America did not become eligible for citizenship until 1943.

An estimated 120,000 people trying to immigrate here in the late nineteenth and early twentieth centuries were deported— sent back to their countries of origin for any number of reasons:

Anti-immigration cartoon from the 1860s. "The Great Fear of the Period: That Uncle Sam May Be Swallowed by Foreigners. The Problem Solved." (Library of Congress, Prints and Photographs Division, LC-DIG-pga-03047)

medical (infectious diseases or poor health), political (anarchists), lack of education, mental illness ("lunacy"), and more. "Now is the time to take greater precautions to differentiate between the good and the bad immigrant," said the Ellis Island commissioner of immigration around 1910. Like so many other native-born Americans of the period, the commissioner was deeply influenced by eugenics and believed that certain types of immigrant would taint the American gene pool. The commissioner argued strenuously in front of Congress that the list of medical exclusions should be expanded. Federal law banned the so-called "feebleminded" from being admitted; they were labeled "mentally unfit" and denied entry into the nation. Terms like "moron," "imbecile," and "idiot" were used as labels to describe various mental deficiencies, or simply the general state of seeming stupid. Increasingly, immigrants were tested for mental defects. The psychologist Henry Goddard oversaw much of this testing, and his results were presented before Congress to show that roughly 40 percent of the Italians, eastern European Jews, and Russians were "mentally deficient." Besides oral testing, the historical record shows that doctors used calipers to measure the circumference of immigrants' heads as a measure of mental fitness.[7]

A literacy requirement for immigration also came to pass in 1917. In 1921, by an overwhelming majority, Congress passed the Emergency Quota Act, establishing national immigration quotas for groups that it considered undesirable. The Supreme Court ruled in 1923 that South Asian Indians should be classified as nonwhite; persons from the Indian subcontinent who had already become U.S. citizens through the naturalization process had their citizenship revoked. Many other laws restricted the ability of Asian people to come to America or live as full citizens here for many decades.

When Congress passed the Immigration Act of 1924 (known as the Johnson-Reed Act) and President Coolidge signed it into law, it targeted southern and eastern European immigrants (largely Italians and Jews), large numbers of whom had immigrated to the United States in prior decades; by contrast, newcomers from northern Europe, Ireland, and England were favored, due to the way the quotas were set up. The quota for new immigrants was, for each country, 2 percent of that country's population in the United States according to the 1890 census. (Moreover, whereas quotas of the past had been based solely on people born outside the United States, the new law traced the national origins of the entire U.S. population, foreign-born and natural-born citizens alike—again, greatly enabling much larger numbers of white people from the British Isles and western Europe in contrast to other parts of the world.) Under the draconian Asian Exclusion Act (part of the 1924 Immigration Act), not only the Chinese but all persons from Asia were completely excluded from immigrating, a provision that greatly angered the Japanese government. As the State Department's own Office of the Historian writes today on its website: "It appeared that the U.S. Congress had decided that preserving the racial composition of the country was more important than promoting good ties with Japan. . . . In all of its parts, the most basic purpose of the 1924 Immigration Act was to preserve the ideal of U.S. homogeneity."[8]

Less than a decade later, the State Department under President Hoover drastically reduced immigration amid the terrible economic and labor crises that characterized the Great Depression, deporting and forcibly repatriating nearly two million Mexican Americans, by some estimates, most of them already naturalized Americans. Americans seemed to want to turn inward during that era; presumably it felt overwhelming to care for the poor already within the nation's borders. After 1940, however, the momentum seemed to shift in the other direction: in that decade, Congress repealed both the Chinese exclusion laws and those against Indian Americans. But the quotas were resurrected in the Immigration and Nationality Act of 1952 (known as the McCarran-Walter Act); President Truman vetoed that act, but Congress overrode his veto. Stepping back to view the big picture, it's clear that both the nation's political leaders and large numbers of its citizens were wrestling with questions of how many and what kinds of foreigners to let in. What could it possibly mean to "welcome the stranger" in such circumstances?

President Truman asked that very question and, in an act of

open resistance to McCarran-Walter, commissioned a report on the impact of U.S. immigration policies. The report was published in early 1953 (while Truman was still president and before Eisenhower was inaugurated later that month) and was aptly named *Whom We Shall Welcome*. It was a title based on words from George Washington penned 170 years earlier, in 1783: "The bosom of America is open to receive not only the Opulent and Respectable Stranger, but the oppressed and persecuted of all Nations And Religions; whom we shall wellcome [*sic*] to a participation of all our rights and previleges [*sic*], if by decency and propriety of conduct they appear to merit the enjoyment."[9] The report's authors were definitive in their view that the national origins criteria driving immigration policy should be abolished. In their words:

> *The national origins system failed in its avowed purpose because it was arbitrary and did not conform to the facts. . . . The national origins system is based on false assumptions, unsubstantiated by physical science, history, sociology, economics, or anthropology.* The Commission found substantial evidence to corroborate the Senate Judiciary Committee statement that many of the considerations which lay behind the passage of the national origins quota law have now become of little significance. *The Commission recommends, therefore, that since the basis of the national origins system is gone, the system itself should go.*[10]

Quite a radical rebuke of the nativism still embedded in U.S. immigration laws at midcentury!

Whom We Shall Welcome exerted real influence on the executive branch of the Eisenhower administration as well as congressional policymakers. Senators working for immigration reform in the 1960s pointed directly to the report's recommendations. President Kennedy, who as a Massachusetts senator had already published a book called *A Nation of Immigrants* and was in fact revising it when he was assassinated, also supported reforming immigration policy to be less nativist. His words: "Every American who ever lived, with the exception of one group, was either an immigrant himself or a descendant of immigrants." And yet, he wrote, practically every wave of immigrant groups provoked xenophobia among those who had been here longer and considered themselves real Americans. "There has always been public sentiment against immigration, or, more accurately, against immigrants," he wrote. "At times this sentiment was only latent, at times it has been manifest, indeed, crudely so. Most often it has been unorganized but in some periods it has been most effectively organized. The usual term for this sentiment is 'nativism' which has been defined as 'the fear of and hostility toward new immigrant groups.'" Still, Kennedy was optimistic that "nativism" would never win: Nativist movements failed, he wrote, "not because the seeds were not there to be cultivated, but because American society is too complex for any movement so narrowly conceived to be politically successful. That they found a response at all should cause us to look more searchingly at ourselves. That the response was at times so great should give cause for alarm."[11]

Finally, in 1965, the forty-year-old quota system based on "national origins" was thoroughly overturned by the Immigration and Nationality Act (known as the Hart-Celler Act). This was during Lyndon Johnson's administration, amid the civil rights movement and the slowly dawning recognition among growing numbers of white Americans of the perniciousness of racism, as well as foreign pressures opposing the discriminatory immigration laws. Hart-Celler removed the emphasis on race in America's immigration laws and instead emphasized family reunification (which critics would come to denounce as "chain migration") and professionals with expert skills. The year before, in his 1964 State of the Union address, Johnson had said: "A nation that was built by the immigrants of all lands can ask those who seek admission, 'What can you do for our country?' But we should not be asking, 'In what country were you born?'"[12] President Johnson signed the act into law in a deeply symbolic ceremony at the foot of the Statue of Liberty. (Incidentally, Congress did add an amendment to the law that added "sexual deviation" as a medical exclusion that would deny entry to immigrants whom they found to exhibit signs of homosexuality; in fact, this provision remained in place until 1990, when Congress withdrew "sexual deviation" from the law.)[13] The law was enacted three years later, in June 1968.

Although Johnson had tried to assuage opponents by saying, at the law's signing, that it was "not a revolutionary bill" and that it would "not affect the lives of millions," the 1965 law has had an enormous impact on the changing ethnic makeup of the country since its passage. Even as the number of immigrants increased— immigration accounted for roughly 15 percent of U.S. population growth in the 1960s; by the 1980s it was 30 percent, and by the early years of the first decade of the twenty-first century, 40 percent—the overwhelming majority of immigrants shifted from Europeans and Canadians to immigrants from Latin American and Hispanic countries and from many different parts of Asia.[14] According to the Pew Research Center, in the last half century (between 1965 and 2015), nearly fifty-nine million immigrants came to the United States, increasing the foreign-born population to 14 percent. Roughly half (51 percent) are Latin American, and one-quarter come from Asia. Projecting ahead, at this rate Pew expects immigrants to account for 88 percent of the U.S. population increase between 2015 and 2065.[15] Still following the Pew analysis, if there had been no immigration after 1965, the nation's citizens would be (as of 2015) about 75 percent white, 14 percent Black, 8 percent Hispanic, and less than 1 percent Asian. As it is, the nation in 2015 was roughly 62 percent white, 12 percent Black, 18 percent Hispanic, and 6 percent Asian.

Naturally, there are those who do not like these changes and want more restrictions on immigration. There are many reasons for this, but the one that they most cite (whether because it's truly their chief concern or because they know it seems more innocent than other, race-based concerns) is jobs. This too fits right in with older anti-immigrant campaigns focusing on jobs.

Unlike other recent administrations, members of President Donald Trump's inner circle—notably senior policy adviser Stephen Miller—overtly stoked a sense of profound urgency and fear when it came to immigration. In early 2019 on *Fox News Sunday*, Miller excoriated President George W. Bush, claiming that illegal border crossings during his presidency doubled from six million to twelve million people and calling this "an astonishing betrayal of the American people." (According to data from the Department of Homeland Security, the number of unauthorized immigrants living in the United States grew by 27 percent during the Bush years.)[16] The chief focus during the Trump administration was twofold: the southern border between the United States and Mexico, and the travel ban (often derided as a "Muslim ban") against citizens of Libya, Yemen, Iran, Somalia, North Korea, Syria, and Venezuela. Miller pushed to end the Deferred Action for Childhood Arrivals program (DACA) that has, since 2012, offered some protections and the ability to work for some people who as children were brought to the United States illegally by their parents. Miller was patently one of the strongest advocates for the notorious "zero tolerance" policy of responding to families caught crossing the border illegally by separating children from their parents, with apparently little effort made to keep adequate records for reuniting them later. The policy was announced in April 2018. As Miller said in June of the same year, "No nation can have the policy that whole classes of people are immune from immigration law or enforcement. . . . It was a simple decision by the administration to have a zero-tolerance policy for illegal entry, period. The message is that no one is exempt from immigration law."[17]

Thousands of immigrant children were separated from their families starting in the summer of 2017, months before the "zero tolerance" policy was announced, prosecuting parents who crossed the border illegally and holding their children in separate quarters. A federal judge later ruled that the government must reunify the families who were separated under the zero-tolerance order—nearly three thousand children before President Trump ended the family separations in June 2018—but no such order required officials to reunify families separated that entire year prior. According to a chilling report released in January 2019 by the inspector general for the Department of Health and Human Services, federal staff did not keep track of the children's parents, and, as the report put it euphemistically, they "faced challenges in identifying separated children."[18] By October 2019, the American Civil Liberties Union had tallied nearly 5,500 children separated from their parents by the Trump administration since July 2017, including toddlers and breastfeeding infants; government data revealed that the federal government held 69,550 migrant children in custody in 2019 alone.[19] The crisis that spurred so many desperate people to migrate to the United States was an emergency facing the people of Honduras, Guatemala, and El Salvador, thousands of whom were trying to escape debilitating poverty and violent crime. Like the "Lost Children" of the Nazi Empire after World War II, the tragedy of those caged or turned away is both individual and collective: Tara Zahra writes that they will "be remembered collectively, as symbols of a collapse: of an American society based on opportunity for newcomers, respect for the family, decency, and human rights."[20]

The July 2018 murder of University of Iowa student Mollie Tibbetts by an undocumented immigrant from Mexico was instantly politicized. The commander in chief and other White House staff repeatedly said her death "should have never happened" and used the killing to condemn Democrats for the nation's "disgrace"—its lax immigration laws and its enabling of a foreign "invasion," an oft-used term.[21] Fears were often stoked about so-called "caravans" of migrants from El Salvador, Honduras, and Guatemala rushing the Mexico-U.S. border. Informed experts on these countries insisted that people were desperate to escape the corruption, violence, and pervasive crime that had cast misery on their lives there. The alt-right claimed that such caravans were funded by George Soros, as seen in this nativist cartoon by the libertarian cartoonist Ben Garrison, long a favorite of alt-right provocateurs such as Alex Jones, Mike Cernovich, and Milo Yiannopoulos.[22] In November President Trump signed a presidential proclamation that halted the routine procedures for seeking asylum for anyone not entering through a designated port of entry. This order went against both U.S. and international law, which allows migrants to seek asylum "whether or not" they do so at a designated entry point. But Miller and his allies still focused on what they saw as the outrage of asylum seekers "gaming the system" by vanishing into the country before their immigration cases could be adjudicated in court. And so, asylum seekers generally were being turned away. As one former Trump administration official said to the *New Yorker*, "[The President and his advisers] don't have any more tools beyond just tightening the screws: separate families, eliminate asylum and due process, turn back people at the border."[23]

In December 2018 and January 2019, a battle over Trump's desire to build a wall across the U.S.-Mexico border brought

"D Day Invasion." Cartoon by Ben Garrison. (© GRRRGRAPHICS.COM)

about the longest government shutdown in U.S. history. Trump-supporting cartoonists like Garrison suggested that Mexican and Latin American would-be immigrants were dirty and wanted "free stuff" and would wreck the U.S. economy. In another provocative cartoon, Garrison played upon the famous words from "The New Colossus," the poem Emma Lazarus wrote in 1883 that was mounted in bronze on the pedestal of the Statue of Liberty: "Give me your tired, your poor, Your huddled masses yearning to breathe free, The wretched refuse of your teeming shore. Send these, the homeless, tempest-tost to me, I lift my lamp beside the golden door." Garrison's version: "Give me your diseased masses of uneducated, unskilled poor wretches yearning for free stuff—all eager to vote for us Democrats!"

A final Garrison cartoon well illustrates the type of anti-immigrant sentiments circulating among the most avid supporters of President Trump's border policies. It referenced a famous

GIVE ME YOUR DISEASED MASSES OF UNEDUCATED, UNSKILLED POOR WRETCHES
YEARNING FOR FREE STUFF ∼ ALL EAGER TO VOTE FOR US DEMOCRATS!

"The Hole Truth. Give Me Your Diseased Masses of Uneducated, Unskilled
Poor Wretches Yearning for Free Stuff—All Eager to Vote for US Democrats!"
Cartoon by Ben Garrison. (© GRRRGRAPHICS.COM)

photograph of Maria Meza, a migrant woman from Honduras,
running from tear gas with her two daughters, both dressed only
in T-shirts and diapers, one barefoot and the other stumbling or
falling, in front of the U.S.-Mexican border wall. After they raced
away from the tear gas and finally stopped, the photographer captured another photo of one of the girls, who had lost her shoes and
was in anguish. Both images captivated many Americans.[24] They
did not captivate Garrison, however, and his response was a cartoon asserting that the photo was staged by "fake news media" in
the form of CNN. Critical to note is the fact that Garrison's harsh
view was not an outlier; to a greater or lesser degree, it represented the views of a considerable segment of the U.S. population,
including so many who still believe a border wall is an essential
component in what will "Make America Great Again."

White evangelicals were a staunchly devoted segment of Trump

A family runs from tear gas as they attempt to cross the border from Tijuana, Mexico, into the United States, 2018. (Kim Kyung Hoon/Reuters Pictures)

"Fake News at the Border. OK. Let's try it again. This time show more fear and fatigue. Remember, you're starving and you just walked over 1,000 miles!" Cartoon by Ben Garrison. (© GRRRGRAPHICS.COM)

supporters. Robert Jeffress, pastor of the fourteen-thousand-member First Baptist Church in Dallas and a member of Trump's closest religious circle, repeatedly defended Trump on a number of Fox News television shows (as well as his own show, regularly broadcast on the Trinity Broadcasting Network). In January 2019, amid the government showdown, Jeffress went on *Lou Dobbs Tonight* on Fox Business Network to defend Trump's wall and his willingness to let the government shut down in order to get it. "The Bible says even heaven itself is gonna have a wall around it," noted Jeffress. "Not everyone is gonna be allowed in." Likewise, in other venues, Jeffress defended the Trump administration's family-separation policies and came to Trump's defense when he ridiculed accepting immigrants from "shithole countries," saying, "Apart from the vocabulary attributed to him, President Trump is right on target in his sentiment." In his white evangelical world, Jeffress was no outlier; the vast majority of his religious cohort likewise supported Trump's restrictionist impulse, scoffing at the notion suggested by some that Jesus himself was a refugee and calling the Democrats immoral for "continu[ing] to try to block this president from performing his God-given task of protecting this nation."[25]

It is instructive to go through these last 100 to 150 years and see how the attitudes of Americans—both ordinary citizens and political leaders—have fluctuated and vacillated over time, how nativist leaders have stoked fear and worked successfully to fracture the American people on how to treat strangers, foreigners who wish to enter the United States. We've never been without nativism in this country. Attitudes toward immigrants—and particularly white attitudes toward brown-skinned immigrants—have been charged with emotion and suspicion consistently over time. Even those who descend from immigrants themselves have frequently been less than enthusiastic about embracing those whom

George Washington called "the oppressed and persecuted of all Nations And Religions; whom we shall welcome." How American citizens, especially but not exclusively white citizens, imagine immigrants—what emotions people feel, what responses these feelings stir up, how people become habituated to care (or not care), to respond (or remain indifferent), how Americans become trained to act toward their would-be neighbors—has critical consequences for our capacity, as a nation, to receive the stranger and offer refuge to the needy and the oppressed.

The concept of "welcoming the stranger" is one that is part of most if not all religious traditions, and as most Americans have had some kind of religious identity it may be worth lingering on that idea a bit. Both the Hebrew Bible and the Christian New Testament stress the ethical importance of welcoming strangers (the Hebrew word, as I understand it, can also be translated as "newcomers" or "aliens" or "resident aliens"). As one Roman Catholic scholar wrote in the early days of the Trump administration, "The Hebrew Bible recognizes that every one of us can be a stranger and, for that very reason, we need to overcome our fear of those who live among us whom we do not know."[26]

Probably the best-known New Testament passage about strangers is from the book of Matthew, chapter 25, verses 31–40. This is a passage describing how Jesus will speak on the Day of Judgment to those who lived correctly according to his teachings (figuratively, the sheep) and those who did not (the goats). To the sheep he says, "Come, you that are blessed by my Father, inherit the kingdom prepared for you from the foundation of the world; for I was hungry and you gave me food, I was thirsty and you gave me something to drink, I was a stranger and you welcomed me, I was naked and you gave me clothing, I was sick and you took care of me, I was in prison and you visited me." Puzzled, the righteous are imagined to answer with confusion at not remembering caring for Jesus in any of these ways, and he responds, "Truly I tell you, just as you did it to one of the least of these who are members of my family, you did it to me."²⁷ Christianity is a wildly diverse religion with many different interpretations, but it's difficult to imagine making a credible argument against the proposition that the teachings embedded here are intended, by the author of the book of Matthew anyway, to be the crux of the Christian life—feeding the hungry, caring for the sick and the poor, welcoming the stranger.

Other religious traditions have their own versions of such teachings to care for others, including outsiders entering one's own community: Judaism teaches that hospitality to strangers is an ethical obligation, a lesson conveyed many times in the Torah, the Talmud, and other Jewish texts. Islam likewise requires the generous welcoming of guests and strangers. And if secular humanist communities have discarded all the trappings of religion that they consider superstition, oppression by patriarchal authorities, and general humbug, responding to the needs and sufferings of strangers is often the very core of what binds them together in community. It surely doesn't take religious belief to want to teach children to care for others and learn to imaginatively put themselves in other people's shoes, as it were, so that they will refrain from biting or hitting or swiping another child's toys.

To welcome the stranger, then, seems to rely in part on practices of empathy: imagining ourselves in their place, as Jesus places himself in the role of the least among us. There are a number of different ways to define and describe empathy, a concept that has received enormous attention from social psychologists, moral philosophers, neuroscientists, and other investigators. A number of researchers today distinguish two kinds of empathy: "Affective empathy" means something like feeling what another person is feeling and feeling that way because of that person's own situation, not one's own. As one author writes: "In seeing a sad face of another and feeling sad oneself, such feeling of sadness should count as genuinely empathic only if one recognizes that in feeling sad one's attention is still focused on the other and that it is not an appropriate reaction to aspects of one's own life. . . . In order for my happiness or unhappiness to be genuinely empathic it has to be happiness or unhappiness about what makes the other person happy [or unhappy]."[28] "Cognitive empathy" means straightforwardly comprehending another person's emotions— reading or identifying them without feeling them. Most of the time, those using the term are using it in the first, affective sense; the moral psychologist Paul Bloom describes the most typical meaning of empathy as "the act of coming to experience the world as you think someone else does," and that is the general meaning here.[29]

There are some problems with empathy. For one thing, a person's empathy is limited by his or her own inability to completely and perfectly grasp anyone else's feelings. Any of us approaches another only by degrees, and the measure of empathy might be how much one truly wants to understand the deep nuances of another person's experience and emotions. For another, as Bloom analyzes in some detail, empathy tends to focus more on specific individuals whose stories others find richly compelling, such as white Americans expressed for the parents of the children murdered at Sandy Hook Elementary School in Newtown, Connecticut, in 2012. Empathy tends to have a narrow here-and-now focus, and it misses the vast numbers of needy people in the world whose stories stay local and unphotographed. It is myopic and tends to reflect the biases of the empathizer: it is, after all, much easier to empathize with people who are close to or similar to us and to those we find appealing and worthy of our care. Empathy can "sway us toward the one over the many," in Bloom's words, and ignores the fact that helping one person today could lead to greater suffering in the future; it "distorts our moral judgments in pretty much the same way that prejudice does."[30]

Some researchers also suggest reasons for believing that, as three political scientists put it, "people are systematically biased in how they experience empathy on a day-to-day basis and tend to display greater empathy toward ingroup members." Elizabeth Simas, Scott Clifford, and Justin Kirkland claim, in other words, that the effects of empathy are far more limited in real life than they may be in the lab experiments that they suggest have resulted in misleadingly positive conclusions. Moreover, they argue, "even when individuals are willing and able to place themselves in the shoes of another, this can actually *increase* conflict by reinforcing negative stereotypes or triggering anger." Bluntly, that is, while empathy clearly has the potential to reduce bias and facilitate generosity across lines of difference such as race or class, in the real world people tend to "seek out environments that minimize contact with dissimilar others and ideas," and plainly the growth of empathy toward ones like us may work with an actual reduction in empathy toward others. Placing this in a political context, according to Simas, Clifford, and Kirkland, "people who are most disposed to feeling empathy may be *more* politically polarized than those who are less prone to experiencing empathy." Turning the usual analysis of political polarization on its head, they claim that polarization is not caused by lack of empathy; it is, rather, "a product of the biased ways in which we experience empathy." It is in this sense that empathy, they conclude, actually fuels partisan polarization rather than diminishing it.[31]

It's important to note, however, that those researchers are describing "dispositional empathy," not the intentional cultivation of a virtue aimed at compassionate response toward others; and they acknowledge at the end that out-group empathy is increased simply by greater contact and shared experiences with others, which is what ethical cultivation of empathy entails. In this sense, their study is narrow in scope and ethically constricted, more of a warning than a verdict on empathy. If anything, their study is an indictment of clustering, not empathy per se. The journalist Jason Marsh of the Greater Good Science Center at UC Berkeley, who has studied the subject at greater length, writes in subtler terms that empathy is "often a vital first step" toward helping others and performing acts of altruism.[32]

Marsh is directly countering the "limits of empathy" argument of the political and cultural commentator David Brooks, who acidly wrote (in 2011) that empathy "has become a way to experience delicious moral emotions without confronting the weaknesses in our nature that prevent us from actually acting upon them." Empirical research conducted over many decades by social psychologists such as Daniel Batson have suggested that empathy often is, in fact, a "prosocial emotion" that motivates prosocial behaviors such as altruism.[33] In imagining empathy as a "delicious moral emotion," Brooks doesn't have the concept right. Empathy is not narcissism; it's practically the opposite of narcissism, since empathy (at least the affective kind) involves feeling a particular emotion on behalf of another person *because* that person feels this way. Empathy is never finished or complete; we don't actually live other people's experiences, after all, and really have no idea what another person's life is like in its complex totality.

Nonetheless, to quote from Marsh's summary of some recent psychological research in this area:

> Studies have found that kids with more empathy are less likely
> to bully. One recent study shows that inducing empathy in white
> people reduces their feelings of prejudice toward African Amer-
> icans and encourages more positive interracial interactions. And

a seminal study . . . looked for commonalities among people who had rescued Jews during the Holocaust; the [researchers] found that the rescuers were deeply empathic—from a young age, they were encouraged by their parents to take other people's perspectives. . . . Research clearly suggests that when we identify with someone, when we see the world through his or her eyes, we're more likely to treat them with kindness—perhaps because they seem more human and their needs feel more real to us.[34]

Certainly, empathy doesn't inevitably prompt altruism; and people who don't empathize with someone can still help out of other motivations—Bloom, for instance, strongly prefers a model of moral action that derives from "rational compassion," a view aligned with that of the utilitarian moral philosopher Peter Singer, among others. By their calculations, morality basically entails doing the most good for the most people as possible, regardless of how "sympathetic" any single individual's situation may be. Since rational compassion bears a close relation to cognitive empathy— and as there is no *inhereent* reason why cognitive empathy should favor one's own kind any more than rational compassion does— empathy as a "vital first step" makes a great deal of sense as a critical value to cultivate in our time.[35]

There is also an argument to be made that the imperative to "welcome the stranger" is specifically an imperative that you must welcome even those with whom you cannot empathize— strangers, not friends, or those who feel like strangers. We must welcome the ones who do not look like us or think like us, or who do not evoke our sympathies. Perhaps what the passage about Jesus putting himself in the role of the prisoner, the sick, and the stranger is urging is to do is both: empathize, as Jesus does, and where we fail to empathize, welcome anyway.

One of the most consistent themes of Barack Obama's writings and speeches has long been empathy, and he likewise uses it in this expansive, more-than-people-like-me way. In one oft-quoted passage from his 2004 keynote address at the Democratic National Convention, early in his national political career, he invoked the caring that stems from empathy:

> If there is a child on the south side of Chicago who can't read, that matters to me, even if it's not my child. If there's a senior citizen somewhere who can't pay for their prescription drugs, and has to choose between medicine and the rent, that makes my life poorer, even if it's not my grandparent. If there's an Arab American family being rounded up without benefit of an attorney or due process, that threatens my civil liberties. . . . It is that fundamental belief—I am my brother's keeper, I am my sister's keeper—that makes this country work. It's what allows us to pursue our individual dreams and yet still come together as one American family.[36]

President Obama repeatedly spoke a warning about one of the greatest dangers he felt the United States faced—an "empathy deficit"—as far back as his 2004 interviews with Oprah Winfrey and Charlie Rose. In his Commencement address to the UMass class of 2006, he said, "Empathy is a quality of character that can change the world—one that makes you understand what your obligations to others are, that they extend beyond the people who look like you and act like you and laugh at the same jokes as you do and live in the same neighborhoods."[37] He continually credited his mother with instilling in him a sense of empathy, and he cited that sense as the reason he chose to become a community organizer on the South Side of Chicago after graduating from college. Over and over again, Obama urged Americans to, as he put it, "make a habit of empathy" for the sake of the nation as well as themselves.

Needless to say, empathy and compassion alone cannot steer citizens through the complex details of policy decisions on which immigrants should be admitted into the United States and which should not. But it can nonetheless offer guidance on remembering and even cherishing the humanity of those desperate enough to break laws against their entry. Would any child choose to be forcibly separated from his or her parents, caged up among caregivers who were sometimes abusive, compelled to sleep on the floor in an icy room without having any idea what would happen next? Would any parent choose to have their children wrenched from them, possibly forever? How much trauma has been inflicted upon people who have fled terribly violent and abusive environments in their homelands? People sometimes think (even if they don't say it out loud), "Well, these parents shouldn't have come here in the first place; they knew what they were risking." But it seems obvious from the stories of immigrants who went through Ellis Island, among so many others, that people don't typically move to a foreign country on a lark; in circumstances that cause people to leave behind their homes and nearly everything they treasure, they are very likely desperate.

Like battles over slavery—and not unrelated to them—battles over migrant "outsiders" have bitterly divided us for generations. Issuing platitudes about this problem won't come anywhere near solving it. Like the official dishonesty and toleration of lies so evident in early twenty-first-century U.S. politics, the indifference expressed by many Americans to the suffering of immigrants, refugees, and asylum seekers has been a solid current in our national discourse for well over a century. So has its opposite, the impulse to care. Cultivating the virtue of empathy requires practicing it and continually striving for it. If empathy is never complete, there is no end to learning it, habituating ourselves to it, correcting ourselves against behaviors that diminish it, and enacting it as an ongoing practice.

3

COURAGE

*Ghosts of Coverture and
the Persistence of Misogyny*

Kamala did you fight for ideals or did you sleep
your way to the top with Willie Brown?

—Tomi Lahren on Twitter, July 31, 2019, addressed
to future Vice President Kamala Harris

IN ADDRESSING RACE AND IMMIGRATION as two major issues
that have fractured the people of the United States, I have tried to
suggest that how Americans narrate history is a crucially important factor in maintaining these divides. And I have argued for
the cultivation of both truthfulness and empathy as necessary,
if insufficient, values or practices needed for a bearable peace.
A third major issue long at the center of our so-called culture wars
is gender. Gender, and in particular women's autonomy over their
bodies and their sexuality, has been a core concern in virtually all
of the major dividing issues since women successfully won the
right to vote in 1920. Telling this history truthfully is critical for
answering one deceptively simple question: Why the long resistance in the United States to women's equality?

Analyzing the past to address this question requires grappling with the protracted reign of misogyny in American life. This is not to suggest that men have indiscriminately hated women throughout U.S. history; while wholesale woman-hating exists, it has been more the exception than the rule in most periods of our past, and very few American men show signs of hating all women. But the emotional condition of woman-hating is not the only or most important way to think about misogyny. Instead, as one counselor puts it, "Misogyny is not an undifferentiated hatred of women, it is a hatred towards women who break the rules."[1] The philosopher Kate Manne has developed this concept quite thoroughly in her book *Down Girl: The Logic of Misogyny*. She critiques the "naïve conception" that misogyny is an emotion or individual psychological state, or that it is hatred of all women purely because they are women. Rather, Manne argues, misogyny is better thought of as a very powerful set of enforcement mechanisms that punish women who go against the rules of patriarchy and reward women who are compliant. Just as there is structural racism in U.S. society, there is structural sexism; misogyny is the coercive apparatus that holds it in place, insisting that women freely provide forms of care and nurture not required of men. Misogyny consists of the hostility women face (from other women, not just men) when they refuse to perform their traditional gender roles. In Manne's words, misogyny "primarily targets women because they are women in a *man's world* (i.e., a historically patriarchal one, among other things) rather than because they are women in a *man's mind*, where that man is a misogynist." It is the "'law enforcement' branch of a patriarchal order, which has the overall function of *policing* and *enforcing* its governing ideology."[2]

Patriarchy is not simply sex role segregation based on the biological fact that women give birth and men do not; it is the presumption that this and other perceived biological differences (whether real or imagined) signify men's superiority over women, with greater freedom, autonomous choice, and power accorded to them and attendant subservience to women. Misogyny presumes a patriarchal social ordering in which men essentially rule over women, occupy positions of authority barred to women, matter more than women, and rely on the care and services of women to meet their needs. At its extreme, it is the world of *The Handmaid's Tale*, enforced through manipulation and psychological torture as well as physical violence up to and including murder; but in the real world it comes in much subtler forms as well, such as the disproportionate attention given to men's sports, starting when boys are quite young; as well as the greatly disproportionate domestic and childrearing labor performed by full-time working mothers over fathers even in progressive marriages in which both partners value an equal division of labor—and the social disapproval visited on women who protest.[3]

The enforcement mechanisms are widely variable, ranging from belittling and humiliating to sexualizing (or desexualizing) to savagely beating, and much in between: it's an extensive spectrum. In Manne's words, these punishments "put women in their place when they seem to have 'ideas beyond their station'" while applauding those women who conform to patriarchal norms: "loving mothers, attentive wives, loyal secretaries, 'cool' girlfriends, or good waitresses" (for example). The "often overlooked mirror image" of misogyny is what Manne calls "himpathy," or the "excessive sympathy sometimes shown toward male perpetrators of sexual violence": her key example is Brock Turner, the Stanford student who was caught sexually assaulting an unconscious young woman but who garnered more sympathy from the judge who sentenced him than his victim did.[4] Under her definition of misogyny, Manne notes, many if not most people, whether male, female, or nonbinary, probably partake of misogynistic social forces and promulgate them as well, even the most egalitarian women and feminist men among us. It's the air we breathe, so to speak, and extremely difficult to escape, however fervently we may wish to do so or assume we have.

Manne's particular definition of misogyny is useful in that to analyze it is not simply to point the finger at all men as the culprits and women as the helpless victims. Women *are* casualties of misogyny, but they are perpetrators of it too, in this model, without thinking of their actions in such terms. As Manne notes, large sectors of "the dominant social class" have "a vested interest in maintaining men's superiority"; but those not of that class have their own vested interests too.[5] It has often been noted that many women may feel that patriarchy offers them protection, and so they resent those seeking to dismantle it—including, often enough, transgendered and nonbinary persons who reject traditional ideals of gender altogether.

Women have, that is, participated aggressively in upholding traditional patriarchal structures or authority and obedience, no less than men. From Phyllis Schlafly and Beverly LaHaye to Laura Ingraham and Ann Coulter, antifeminist women have lambasted feminism and mocked women who have fought for equal pay and equal rights. Some have indulged in so-called "slut-shaming," or sexual scapegoating, by accusing other women of gaining power by "sleeping their way to the top," as right-wing pundit Tomi Lahren accused California senator (and later U.S. Vice President) Kamala Harris of doing during the Democratic primaries in 2019.[6] Women might mock other women with humiliating sexist slurs, as when, amid President Clinton's sex scandals of the late 1990s, columnist Maureen Dowd ruthlessly jeered Monica Lewinsky as "ditsy" with an "immunity from brains," a "dingbat," "girlish," lovesick albeit a crazed stalker, a "red-blooded predator" aggressively seeking both sex and profit, and "too tubby to be in the high school 'in' crowd."[7] Women who do not work outside the home and occupy the traditional domestic roles of wife and mother might criticize working women who rely on childcare. Women might—women *do*—criticize other women's looks or clothes as not pretty, not stylish, not sexy, too sexy, or any number of other things. Witness the lampoonish, *Mad Magazine*–style cover of Kate O'Beirne's 2005 antifeminist book *Women Who Make the World Worse,* topped by Rush Limbaugh's endorsement: a toothy Hillary Clinton leers menacingly and wears a man's suit; the proverbial bra burns from a pole in the head of an addled-looking Jane Fonda; Ruth Bader Ginsburg scowls goggle-eyed beneath a sign panning men; Sarah Jessica Parker's Carrie Bradshaw lusts for gaudy stilettos; and all four women are rendered unflatteringly, to say the least.

Misogyny is not merely the preoccupation of a few rejected, disgruntled men like Elliot Rodger, whose self-proclaimed loathing for women fueled a killing spree in California in 2014. It structures micro- and macro-level choices women make every day about how to present themselves in the world, how to behave around men, how to treat women and nonbinary people who have made a conscious decision to reject traditional gender norms altogether. It is far more pervasive than hatred of women generally or of certain women in particular, and yet that pervasiveness can make it seem invisible, silent, and nearly impossible to root out.

Like racism, and like ambivalent attitudes toward foreigners wishing to migrate to America, the structures of gender hierarchy have a long and deep history. Puritan conceptions of womanhood in early New England conceived women as having vile natures, helping to explain why so many more women than men were accused

Cover of Kate O'Beirne's *Women Who Make the World Worse*. (Penguin Random House, LLC)

of witchcraft during the Salem episode, why they frequently confessed, and why the accused often implicated other women with allegations of witchcraft.[8] This presumption of women's greater evil and propensity to sin and tempt others into sin fluctuated over time, and at times women who best conformed to images of ideal Christian femininity (such as reigned during the Victorian era) were perceived as more prone to holiness and closer to God. But not until the twentieth century did women gain anything even close to equal rights with men; patriarchal assumptions of gender hierarchy were embedded in the common law that English settlers brought over to America. For much of the eighteenth and nineteenth centuries, the doctrine of coverture meant that a married woman's rights were suspended and essentially owned by her husband: she could not own property, for instance, or enter into contracts under her own name. She was forbidden from seeking an education without her husband's permission or earning a salary for herself; any wages earned had to be turned over to her husband. She was essentially not seen as a person apart from her husband; they were considered as one, and the "one" really meant him. Abigail Adams's famous 1776 anticoverture appeal to her husband, John, to "Remember the Ladies" when creating the law code for the new nation. "Your Sex are Naturally Tyrannical," she wrote, and "all Men would be tyrants if they could"—was met with the future president's sneering response calling her "saucy" for her request and glibly noting, "I cannot but laugh."[9]

Reforms to coverture occurred beginning in the nineteenth century, but the common law continued to uphold gender norms in visible ways. As a Kentucky court wrote in 1922: "At common law the husband and wife are under obligation to each other to perform certain duties. The husband is to bring home the bacon, so to speak, and to furnish a home, while on the wife devolved the duty to keep said home in a habitable condition." The division between market labor and household labor was not an equal one, however, since, the legal scholar Reva Siegel writes, wives could not "assert claims on assets that accrued from their work in the household setting. . . . A wife might claim rights in her market wages, but . . . the value of a 'wife's work'—her household labor—remained a husband's by marital right."[10] Laws pertaining to the rights of wives and asset division upon divorce have gradually changed over time, but the assumption that participation in the market economy is more valuable than domestic work remains unchanged, shored up by law and attitudes alike. In this and other ways, the American historian Catherine Allgor writes, "The ghost of coverture has always haunted women's lives and continues to do so."[11]

The waves of European immigrants coming to America in the nineteenth and early twentieth centuries not infrequently brought with them customs of strict gender hierarchy. In her social realist fiction based largely on real-life experiences, the Russian immigrant novelist Anzia Yezierska wrote poignantly about the conditions of some Orthodox Jewish women in the Lower East Side ghettos, subjected to the brutal rule of their husbands and to the view that women were less human than men. In *Bread Givers,* the recently immigrated Reb Smolinsky says to his daughter Sara: "A woman's highest happiness is to be a man's wife, the mother of a man's children. You're not a person at all." Elsewhere, Sara reflects on his worldview:

> The prayers of his daughters didn't count because God didn't listen to women. Heaven and the next world were only for men. Women could get into Heaven because they were wives and daughters of men. Women had no brains for the study of God's Torah, but they could be the servants of men who studied the Torah. Only if they cooked for the men, and washed for the men, and didn't nag or curse the men out of their homes; only if they let the men study the Torah in peace, then, maybe, they could push themselves into Heaven with the men, to wait on them there.

As Sara grows up and attempts to live a more autonomous life than her father wished, she eventually learns to pity him, writing: "Then suddenly the pathos of this lonely old man pierced me. In a world where all is changed, he alone remained unchanged—as tragically isolate as the rocks. All that he had left of life was his fanatical adherence to his traditions."[12]

Similarly, in his prize-winning history, Robert Orsi has written about the pitiless gender hierarchies among Italian immigrant families in the early twentieth century and the cultivation of women's utter dependence on the husbands who routinely beat them. The heavy expectations making up the definition of a "good woman" within the *domus* (the home) were harsh; they "trapped and bound women." Orsi continues:

> The good woman was a hard and uncomplaining worker who slaved from morning to night in and on behalf of the domus; she rose long before everyone else and was still awake when the last male drifted off to sleep at night. A good woman felt uncomfortable outside the domus; an extreme statement of this isolation was the insistence among many male immigrants that their wives not learn English and the pride among many women at not having done so after many years in the United States. A good woman did not know how to leave the neighborhood and never learned anything about public transportation. A good woman was utterly loyal to her husband and children; she would sacrifice "everything" for them, as the popular expression put it. She overlooked and covered over her husband's faults. She was humble, submissive, obedient. And above all, she was silent; as men and women remember their mothers, these women are surrounded by a great and deep silence.[13]

The very turmoil of the Italian immigration experience and the fierce pressures to assimilate quickly to the new world, Orsi shows, made gender relations within the home all the more fraught: men who felt they had little power in this strange new America exerted their power all the more ferociously among their families. The man of the house ruled; the wife, according to the Italian ideal, obeyed.

In other conditions of relative powerlessness and systematic discrimination, African American women too encountered obstacle after obstacle to equality with African American men. Black women's club and church activity in the late nineteenth and early twentieth centuries was a "struggle for gender self-determination" and "self-representation," writes the historian Evelyn Brooks Higginbotham. Women such as the civil rights activist Nannie Helen Burroughs decried women's subservient position in Black Baptist churches and spoke of the "righteous discontent" that spurred so many of them to press for a more active role and presence there and in the wider society beyond. White racism hindered their participation in the public sphere more than Black sexism did, but these women did face strong resistance by Black Baptist men to their quest for women's rights within the denomination. Far greater misogynistic forces loomed over them outside the African American community; the feminist scholar Moya Bailey has coined the word "misogynoir" to describe the intersection of anti-Black racism and misogyny in Black women's lives. White men's rape of Black women after Emancipation may not have been as commonplace as it was during slavery, but neither was it rare. Once again, a clear gender hierarchy structured their lives, and there could be real consequences for those who stepped out of their place.[14]

A movement for women's rights, and in particular the right to vote, emerged in the mid-nineteenth century and accelerated into the early twentieth; it would later be termed first-wave feminism. Though the visible public leadership was dominated by white women, and the movement shot through with racist assumptions of Black inferiority, many African American women played a critical role as well, often through local churches and other institutions; Sojourner Truth was an influential leader, as was Burroughs, and other notable trailblazers included Frances Ellen Watkins Harper, Anna Julia Cooper, and Ida B. Wells-

Barnett, among other Black leaders. Many were active in abolitionist and antiracism activism alongside women's rights, and they were vocal in condemning the racism pervasive in white suffrage circles; as Harper said to attendees of the Eleventh National Women's Rights Convention in 1866: "We are all bound up together in one great bundle of humanity, and society cannot trample on the weakest and feeblest of its members without receiving the curse in its own soul. . . . You white women speak here of rights. I speak of wrongs. . . . I tell you that if there is any class of people who need to be lifted out of their airy nothings and selfishness, it is the white women of America."[15] Harper and other Black suffragists insisted that the brutal racism African Americans endured every day should not be separated from the sexism white suffragists preferred to confront.

As the suffrage question gained increasing support across the country, many forces arrayed against it, arguing that women's participation in politics would destroy their true nature and threaten civilization. Critics argued that women's full equality would lead to sexual debauchery, women's abandonment of their husbands and children, and the demise of marriage. Women would be *degraded* by receiving equal rights, many insisted, and their morals would be destroyed. A rather low view of women's character drove such thinking: without full oversight by a husband in authority over the wife, a woman would simply devolve into a profoundly immoral, narcissistic figure, devoid of love and concern for others. Antisuffrage activists also warned of the misery that suffrage would bring, not only for husbands and children but also for women, who would be isolated in a dismal cocoon that was no freedom at all. And in the southern states, antisuffrage activists raised the specter of African American women voting alongside whites and the prospect of what the *Richmond Evening Journal* reviled as "colored rule": Mildred Rutherford of the United

Daughters of the Confederacy told the Georgia legislature, "Woman's suffrage comes from the North and the West and from women who do not believe in state's rights and who wish to see negro women using the ballot," while the *Richmond Times-Dispatch* cautioned ominously that allowing women to vote "would double the number of uncertain and dangerous votes and put the balance of political power in the hands of 165,000 colored women."[16]

Antisuffrage cartoons of the period also showed the horrors conceived if women were to leave the house and expect men to do some of the childcare and housework—a world in disarray. A cartoon published in *Life* magazine in 1912 showed a miserable woman forsaking love, marriage, children, and home to achieve suffrage, which would be accompanied by strife, anxiety, and loneliness.[17] "Everybody Works But Mother—She's a Suffragette" read a sign in another, differently messaged antisuffrage cartoon, which showed a desolate-looking husband in an apron washing clothes with a tub and washboard, cat and baby at his feet. "I want to vote, but MY WIFE WON'T LET ME," howled the woebegone caption. Equally pitiful was the apron-bound man holding a set of screaming twin babies as his mannish-looking wife marched coldly out to vote on "Election Day!" Even the cat stared in horror, for women like this were callous and coldly non-nurturing. Roles will be dreadfully reversed if women get the vote, these cartoons warned; women will behave as men, and men will be forced to become women—plainly, a terrible fate.

The suffrage movement did eventually prevail over its foes, with no mass child abandonments or gender role reversals reported. The Nineteenth Amendment was ratified on August 18, 1920, after Tennessee helped it clear the final hurdle. It was a monumental gain for American women to have achieved the right to vote in all federal and state elections—white women, at least, for while many African American women marched and fought

"Looking Backward," 1912. An antisuffrage cartoon by Laura E. Foster shows the misery that would ensue for women once they had the right to vote. (Everett Collection Inc/Alamy Stock Photo)

for suffrage despite the racism of white suffragists, and while the amendment applied as much to Black women as white, many states adopted laws to prevent Black women and men from voting. Literacy tests, poll taxes, and other Jim Crow tactics of intimidation were widely employed in the South to put the ballot box out of reach for people of color, until the passage of the Voting Rights Act in 1965 invalidated such restrictions.[18] But notwithstanding the prodigious significance of women's suffrage, on its own it could hardly upend the gender hierarchy structuring so much of American life. Misogyny—the deep systemic structures of gender

"I Want to Vote, but My Wife Won't Let Me." Postcard, 1909. (The Protected Art Archive/Alamy Stock Photo)

SUFFRAGETTE SERIES Nº II.

EVERYBODY WORKS BUT MOTHER SHE'S A SUFFRAGETT

I WANT TO VOTE, BUT
MY·WIFE·WONT·LET·ME

and the punishments for women who defied them—retained its powerful force.

Reactionary resistance to the quest for women's equality was ongoing. Soon after the passage of the Nineteenth Amendment, women's rights activists drafted a new amendment to expand women's rights beyond the vote, first dubbing it the Lucretia Mott amendment after the famous suffragist and abolitionist. In 1923, suffrage movement leader Alice Paul launched a campaign, and Kansas Republican senator Charles Curtis introduced what was

"Election Day!" Anti-suffrage cartoon by E. W. Gustin, 1909. (Digitally colored by Granger, NYC)

now called the Equal Rights Amendment (ERA) into Congress in December of that year.[19] The wording of the proposed amendment read thus: "Men and women shall have equal rights throughout the United States and in every place subject to its jurisdiction. Congress shall have power to enforce this article by appropriate legislation." Though introduced numerous times in subsequent years, many progressives opposed it, believing that strict equality of treatment would invalidate special protections, that is, the protective labor laws that social reformers had managed to establish on behalf of women and children, which treated women as weaker and vulnerable to exploitation such as poor compensation, long hours that interfered with childcare, and unsafe working conditions during pregnancy. The labor activist Florence Kelley, who had worked hard for suffrage, condemned the ERA as "topsy-turvy feminism," insisting that "women cannot achieve true equality with men by securing identity of treatment under the law"; ending special protections for women was contrary to their best interest.[20] Not until the late 1960s did the ERA become a feminist cause célèbre and opposition to the amendment a badge of conservativism.

The birth control movement that was spearheaded by Margaret Sanger in the first half of the twentieth century also reaped vehement opposition, particularly from special interest groups arguing that access to contraception was corrupting for women. Starting in the 1920s, Patrick Joseph Hayes, the archbishop of New York, became a fiercely tenacious critic of the movement, working both publicly and behind the scenes to sabotage the efforts of Sanger and other activists. To Catholic leaders' eyes, Sanger's birth control efforts were turning women into selfish, materialistic creatures who cared more about sexual pleasure and their own leisure than about bearing as many children as God would send. Sanger deemed this misogyny and condemned both the church and the nation's legal apparatus for robbing women of their sexual rights, arguing that women must have control over their own bodies. Still more, she wrote: "The church has always been opposed to the progress of women on the ground that it would lead her to immorality. We ask the church now to reverse its method of keeping women moral by fear and give them a higher morality based upon knowledge."[21] Catholic criticisms of Sanger and the birth control movement relentlessly evoked gender roles and the supposed degradations that accrued to women who used contraceptives; early Catholic opponents rarely cited masses of unborn children, as later anti-abortion activists would. And rightly: Sanger herself spoke publicly against abortion over and over again; the later cartoonish depiction of her as wanting to murder babies and exterminate the Black race is patently false.[22]

During World War II, hundreds of thousands of American women entered the paid workforce for the first time, to fill jobs left open by men headed to the battlefields: the female labor force increased by 50 percent between 1940 and 1945, growing by about seven million even as the male labor force decreased by nearly nine million.[23] By 1945, 34 percent of all adult women were employed outside the home.[24] There was a flurry of women's rights activity at this time as well. Interest in the ERA briefly revived, and the language was rewritten to say: "Equality of rights under the law shall not be denied or abridged by the United States or by any state on account of sex." Once the war ended in 1945 and the surviving men came home, some women lost their jobs and returned to full-time domestic life. An era of consolidated gender hierarchy ensued in the 1950s, a period of profound national fear when the threats of nuclear war and Communism hung thick in the air. The marriage rate soared, and couples married very young, often just out of high school or during college, and most started having children right away. White women's roles were strictly circumscribed to the happy housewife and mother, increasingly out in the suburbs somewhere away from the cities that were home to growing numbers of African Americans—the "white flight" that did untold damage to cities in many parts of the country.

In this era of heightened conservatism in white America, the rule of husbands was basically a given. "Show her it's a man's world," urged the men's clothier Van Heusen in 1951, pressing the reader to purchase jaunty-looking ties in "brand new man-talking, power-packed patterns that tell her it's a man's world . . . and make her so happy it is." In the ad, the wife kneels before her husband as she places a piping hot breakfast around his idle lap in bed, her head tilted upward pleadingly like a supplicant seeking the approval of her master. And although the man is half under

"Show Her It's a Man's World." Print advertisement for Van Heusen ties, 1951.

the sheets, a location in which nakedness or pajamas would be expected, his upper half is nattily dressed in the day's work shirt and tie, hands clasped behind his head in a cocksure "King of his domain" pose above his female helpmeet.

Not everyone liked this domestic arrangement, needless to say, and the 1960s saw the emergence of feminism's so-called second wave. The federal government approved "the pill" in 1960, so that women could control their reproductive lives more easily than ever before. Betty Friedan published *The Feminine Mystique* in 1963; a critique of the happy housewife archetype, it was a huge bestseller that helped inspire a national upswell of women's rights activism. The Civil Rights Act of 1964 included Title VII, a federal law banning employers from discriminating against workers on the basis of several criteria that included sex as well as race, color, religion, and national origin. In the summer of 1966, a major conference on the status of women took place in Washington, D.C., after which a group of women including Friedan formed a new organization that would be called the National Organization for Women, or NOW for short. In 1967, NOW resurrected the ERA by putting it on its Bill of Rights for Women. This plus the general turmoil of this era, which also included milestones in the civil rights movement, protests against the Vietnam War, and much else, may have seemed shattering to traditional gender roles; but many of the changes would turn out to be more cosmetic than revolutionary, thanks especially to a surge of antifeminist activism.

Campaigning against women's equality, and building a mighty fortress for misogyny, were a number of ultraconservative Christian leaders who were assembling the foundation for what would be called the Religious Right. Chieftess among them was Phyllis Schlafly, a traditionalist Catholic and Goldwater Republican who fought feminism from the early 1970s until her death in 2016 at the age of ninety-two. The ERA passed the House of Representatives in 1971 and the Senate in March 1972, at which point Schlafly organized a group she called STOP ERA to do exactly that (STOP was an acronym for Stop Taking Our Privileges). The constitutional amendment needed the ratification of thirty-eight states, and Schlafly determined not to let that happen. The crux of her argument was that the ERA would "deprive the American woman of many of the fundamental special privileges we now enjoy, and especially the greatest rights of all: 1) NOT to take a job, 2) to keep her baby, and 3) to be supported by her husband."[25] Privileges also meant protections, she claimed, and she saw these as offering real power to women: the titles for two of her books published in this period were *The Power of the Positive Woman* (1977) and *The Power of the Christian Woman* (1981). But her critics viewed this antifeminist approach as promoting a form of captivity: as one historian later wrote: "Phyllis Schlafly's entire case against the ERA revolved around women's continuing need for male protection. . . . But feminists saw Schlafly persuading women to connive in their own subordination, and understood this dynamic as lying at the heart of women's continuing oppression."[26] The ERA failed to win ratification by a three-state margin by the time the deadline arrived in 1982, and virtually all observers credited Schlafly's organizing genius with the defeat.

In the same years that the ERA was being so hotly contested, the long American battle over women's reproductive rights was gaining new steam as well. The Supreme Court, in its 1973 decision in *Roe v. Wade,* had decriminalized most abortions at a time when a clear majority of Americans supported women's legal right to abortion. The court's decision initially received strong support from liberals and conservatives alike, including conservative evangelicals; but Catholic activists such as Schlafly joined with fundamentalist Protestant leaders Jerry Falwell, Pat Robertson, Beverly LaHaye, and others to shift evangelical opinion to the anti-abortion side—and succeeded with a vengeance. They founded and led the activist political organizations Eagle Forum (Schlafly), Moral Majority (Falwell), Christian Coalition (Robertson), and Concerned Women for America (LaHaye), all of which focused on abortion and a matrix of related gender- and sexuality-related issues—such as homosexuality (they opposed it) and traditional hierarchical marriage (they supported it)—along with other conservative religious causes such as prayer in the public schools. Their success assisted mightily in getting Ronald Reagan elected president in 1980 (and again in 1984) as well as persuading untold numbers of Americans that there was only one Christian position on abortion, and that was to see it as murder, not a woman's right or even an unfortunate procedure that nonetheless was sometimes the best and most appropriate choice.

Since women's ability to participate fully and equally in the U.S. workforce requires them to be able to control when and how many children they have, the vast majority of feminists viewed access to contraception and abortion as a kind of litmus test regarding attitudes toward women's rights: those who support women's full equality ought, in this view, to support generous policies favoring reproductive rights, including federal government funding of abortion (one of the most controversial topics in this highly contentious issue). Pro-choice feminists studied the panoply of concerns that typically accompanied anti-abortion activism, and many concluded that those calling themselves pro-life were, at heart, misogynists who believed in male superiority and gender inequality even if they knew better than to say it out loud. Pro-life advocates typically belonged to churches that would not ordain women to senior leadership—the Roman Catholic Church, the Southern Baptist Convention, and other conservative groups—so it was easy to see that they supported, or at the very least tolerated, hierarchical antifeminist church structures. Opposition to abortion appeared to many feminists to be one more sign of wholesale opposition to women's rights, with the exception of those Catholic feminists who held abortion to be murder (albeit justifiable in exceptional circumstances such as rape or danger to the mother's life).

The labor market was consistently an arena of conflict over women's rights: lawsuits over such issues as employment discrimination, maternity leave, and pay equity clarified the law in many cases, and legislatures did their part. In 1991, sexual harassment in the workplace erupted into public view when Anita Hill's charges against her former boss, Clarence Thomas, were nationally televised during his Supreme Court confirmation hearings. Her claims told of lurid details and highly improper behavior on Thomas's part, most memorably (and repulsively) a joke about finding a pubic hair on his Coke can—all of which he furiously denied, calling the proceedings "a high-tech lynching." This high-profile case could have killed his hopes; instead, Thomas was narrowly confirmed to the court on which he has served for more than a quarter century.

Thomas had been a favorite among ultraconservatives, and many angrily blamed feminists for his mistreatment: the evangelical leader Chuck Colson excoriated the "militant feminism" generated by a "diabolical source" combating Thomas, and he blasted feminism for undermining "the very notion of what it means to be a man, what it means to be a woman." Rush Limbaugh reviled Hill's supporters and other feminists as "femi-Nazis" and bemoaned "the extent to which feminists and their political allies are willing to go to advance their proabortion, militant leftist, antimale agenda." Rosalie Silberman disparaged Hill's supporters as "extremists" and worked with other conservative women to turn a group called Women for Judge Thomas into the Independent Women's Forum, calling itself a "conservative alternative to feminist tenets" that promoted "equity feminism" (a term popularized by Christina Hoff Sommers) over the prevailing feminism of what some called New Feminists. Thomas's nightmarish ordeal proved to them all that men were the real victims, while feminists—the women who refused their traditional female role—were the persecutors.[27]

Supporters of Thomas were still smarting in 1992, when the Democratic primaries heated up ahead of the presidential election. Allegations came to light in January that the primary candidate Bill Clinton had engaged in a twelve-year affair with a woman named Gennifer Flowers, and Bill and his wife, Hillary, went on the CBS news program *60 Minutes* to refute these charges. Amid their defense, Hillary Clinton defended her support of Bill in feminist terms, saying: "I'm not sitting here some little woman standing by my man like Tammy Wynette. I'm sitting here because I love him and I respect him." This garnered a significant public backlash against her, including an angry statement from Wynette, who said Hillary's remark insulted millions (Clinton apologized). A few weeks later, Clinton riled up many people again when, defending her career as an attorney, she said, "I suppose I could have stayed home and baked cookies and had teas, but what I decided to do was to fulfill my profession, which I entered before my husband was in public life." The media did not report what she said after that, which was, "The work that I have done as a professional, as a public advocate, has been aimed in part to assure that women can make the choices that they should make—whether it's full-time career, full-time motherhood, or some combination." A national furor ensued, and the soundbite "I suppose I could have stayed home and baked cookies" made her a widely controversial figure among observers who believed it insulted stay-at-home wives: a New Jersey voter wrote to *Time* magazine, "If I ever entertained the idea of voting for Bill Clinton, the smug bitchiness of his wife's comment has nipped that notion in the bud." And a Wisconsin woman wrote: "I resent the implication that those of us who stay at home just bake cookies. We hardly have the time!" The image of an arrogant Hillary Clinton created in the media by these remarks would haunt her for years to come.[28]

Two years later, Paula Jones sued President Bill Clinton for another incident of unscrupulous sexually harassing behavior. Like Hill's charges against Thomas, Jones's allegations sounded highly credible to many women—but this time, instead of targeting an antifeminist conservative, the contentions focused on a man whom American feminists had voted for and considered a friend to causes such as reproductive rights and equal rights for women. Years of back-and-forth ensued, coloring the remainder of Clinton's two terms.

Hill and Jones both survived the unwanted spotlight their ordeals with famous men shined upon them, but the contempt and cruelty hurled their way was brutal. Amid the controversy over Hill's 1991 testimony, Republican supporters of Thomas publicly accused her of "erotomania," a paranoid delusion that another person is in love with oneself despite there being no evidence of such. Political operative David Brock called her "a little bit nutty and a little bit slutty," a vile misogynist line widely echoed. Asked about Jones, campaign strategist James Carville was even more vicious, replying, "Drag a hundred-dollar bill through a trailer park, you never know what you'll find." Clinton supporters gleefully joined the sadistic pileup, mocking Jones as a "bimbo" and "trailer park trash." Both women endured scores of harassing phone calls, malicious cards and letters, unwanted confrontations with paparazzi and accosting strangers, and much else besides.

And even all of that paled in comparison to the collective dehumanization of Monica Lewinsky. The White House intern, who was all of twenty-four years old when her affair with Clinton was publicly revealed in 1998, instantly became "the most humiliated person in the world" and "the first person whose global humiliation was driven by the Internet." Women mocked her no less than men, as we saw in Dowd's acid words. Lewinsky would recall years later: "I was branded as a tramp, tart, slut, whore, bimbo, and, of course, 'that woman.' . . . The public humiliation was excruciating. Life was almost unbearable."[29] Like Hill and Jones (presuming their truthfulness), Lewinsky was viciously shamed by the flagrant sexual misconduct of a man in power over her who lied and then let her be painted as the villain, the scarlet woman who became famous for a sexual act she performed *on him*.[30] Meanwhile, just as Thomas got his Supreme Court seat, Clinton's humiliating impeachment by the House of Representatives was followed by the Senate's acquittal and a return to his job, and eventually a lengthy and lucrative retirement.

In the pre-#MeToo 1990s, there seemed to be, in fact, a great deal of sympathy for men accused of bad behavior, among women as much as men, as well as a high degree of aversion to women who complained about their unequal treatment in the United States. A wave of antifeminism texts hit the scene, penned by women who had little in common with Phyllis Schlafly religiously or politically; they ran in more intellectual and even liberal circles, sometimes universities, but shared some of Schlafly's disgust for "victim feminism." As Alyson Cole details in *The Cult of True Victimhood,* this spate of antivictim bestsellers included a number of popular books by women convinced "that women are no longer oppressed as a group, and that their progress as individuals is not impeded by the women's movement"; their books denounced what they saw as "victim feminism." These included Rene Denfeld's *The New Victorians: A Young Woman's Challenge to the Old Feminist Order* (1995), Christina Hoff Sommers's *Who Stole*

Feminism? How Women Have Betrayed Women (1994), Camille Paglia's Sex, Art, and American Culture (1992), Katie Roiphe's The Morning After: Sex, Fear, and Feminism on Campus (1993), Naomi Wolf's Fire with Fire: The New Female Power and How It Will Change the 21st Century (1993), and Elizabeth Fox-Genovese's Feminism Is Not the Story of My Life: How Today's Feminist Elite Has Lost Touch with the Real Concerns of Women (1996), among others. These writers described themselves as feminists—in fact, the *real* feminists. In contrast, those feminists from NOW and working in women's studies departments had ruined whatever had once been good about feminism and made women feel victimized, they argued (hence Cole refers to them as "anti-'victim-feminists,'" or AVFers).[31]

The books looked at different areas, but the primary complaint was consistent. As Roiphe put it, feminist analysis "transforms perfectly stable women into hysterical, sobbing victims." Christina Hoff Sommers was similarly caustic: "It used to be fun to be a feminist," she declared. "Now . . . it means male-bashing, it means being a victim, and it means being bitter and angry." Paglia condemned feminism for its "hysterical moralism and prudery," while Wolf argued that it told women they were "beleaguered, fragile, intuitive angels" who should "seek power through an identity of powerlessness."[32] Fox-Genovese, who mentioned Hillary Clinton twice and both times referred to her "cookies" remark, objected that the problem of antiwoman violence had been "wildly exaggerated" and that feminists "have turned a worthy campaign for equity, justice, and common decency into an assault on all manifestations of masculinity."[33] Over and over again, these writers chastised mainstream feminists for decreasing rather than increasing women's recognition of their own power as well as laying too much blame at the feet of men ("peak himpathy," Manne might scoff).[34] Whereas Schlafly had opposed women's equality on the grounds that it reduced women's station from the special privileges they otherwise enjoyed, these writers endorsed women's equality and declared that it had already been achieved, rendering mainstream feminism an indulgence for spoiled crybabies.

These and similar battles over women's equal rights continued to rage on into the early decades of the twenty-first century. Women fighting for equal rights continued to reap scorn as whiny bitches and brutal predators, and their opponents cast men (as well as conservative, traditionalist women) as their prey. More generally, the era of the 2000s and the 2010s—which witnessed the marked transition in U.S. presidential administrations from George W. Bush to Barack Obama to Donald Trump—staged an extraordinary array of events that made it close to impossible to deny the forces of misogyny still driving many segments of American culture. The growing visibility of transgender people reaped backlash, particularly toward nonbinary people and notably toward trans women, a reaction that has been termed *transmisogyny*. The reaction to Caitlyn Jenner, who was assigned male at birth and won international acclaim in the 1970s as the champion decathlete Bruce Jenner, was a case in point. Jenner was a visible member of the extended Kardashian empire, with wife, Kris; stepdaughters, Kim, Kourtney, and Khloé, and stepson, Rob; and daughters, Kendall and Kylie. When, in April 2015, she came out as a trans woman on the ABC news program *20/20,* many showed support; but some comedians and media commentators used her transition for cruel laughs, scorning Jenner for becoming more feminine and straining (as they saw it) to be beautiful. The derision thrown at Jenner for not looking glamorous enough, not quite measuring up to "real" womanhood, not occupying the female role: this was its own special form of misogyny. It fit in line with a number of contemporaneous state battles over transgender bathrooms and allowing trans people to use the restrooms of their chosen gender identity rather than their birth sex, in which the opposition's chief argument was that trans women were *really* men and posed a danger, if allowed into the women's room, of molesting young girls.[35]

The ultimate exhibit of public misogyny turned out to be the 2016 race between Trump and Hillary Clinton, when the choice could not have been starker. Trump was a real estate magnate and reality TV star known for philandering, and he had no political experience whatsoever; whereas Clinton was a Yale-trained lawyer who spent years working alongside her husband in politics, later serving for eight years in the Senate before resigning in the middle of her second term to become U.S. secretary of state. Trump was in every way the antifeminist candidate, while Clinton embodied mainstream feminism. For instance, Trump promised to slash government funding for the reproductive rights organization Planned Parenthood and asserted that "there should be some kind of punishment" for women who had abortions (though later the president claimed he meant punishment for doctors who perform abortions, if the procedure were outlawed); Clinton was pro-choice. Trump swore to take down the many women who called him out for sexual harassment and assault, and he was caught on tape saying he liked to grab women "by the pussy"; Clinton represented herself, with evidence to back it up, as a defender of women's rights. Again and again, on issues of racism, immigration, and misogyny, Trump and Clinton offered utterly distinctive choices.

And yet. Throughout the race, internet, television, and print media all teemed with criticisms of Clinton's supposed "unlikability," her "shrill" style, and her "abrasive" voice. Mainstream journalists repeatedly, and often uncritically, focused on topics such as "the deep disgust for Hillary Clinton that drives so many evangelicals to support Trump."[36] Many people were apparently still infuriated by her 1992 "I suppose I could have stayed home and baked cookies" remark; she had been roundly called a "feminazi" and a "bitch" in hard-line conservative circles for years. Tweets calling her these names as well as "witch," "slut," and "cunt" became par for the course as the election approached.[37]

The T-shirts and campaign trappings at Trump rallies were gleefully saturated with manic, often sexually explicit misogyny. One shirt—"Donald Trump: Finally Someone with Balls"— managed pithily to insult Clinton and Obama at once. "Don't Be a Pussy—Vote for Trump" and "Donald FUCKING Trump" invoked an outraged masculinity implying that real men vote Trump. Grown men as well as high school boys who were at most infants during Bill Clinton's presidency sported T-shirts saying, "Hillary Sucks But Not Like Monica." Widely available buttons and bumper stickers insulted Clinton's body—"KFC Hillary Special: 2 Fat Thighs, 2 Small Breasts . . . Left Wing," said one—and called Clinton "bitch," "tramp," "cunt," and more, moving far beyond the bounds of presidential sloganeering throughout U.S. history. "Feminists Are Sluts! Proverbs 5:5," read one, referring to an ominous biblical verse about the dangers of a "loose woman" whose "feet go down to death."[38] Some trafficked in violent fantasies against her: "SPANK ME" appeared on one set of posters under a famous image of Clinton; even more shocking was another T-shirt captioned, "I Wish Hillary Had Married OJ," implying the wish for her brutal murder à la Nicole Brown Simpson.

Women were full and enthusiastic participants in this explicit misogyny directed against Hillary Clinton. Many gleefully insulted her body or her voice, condemned her for a supposed lack of nurture and "relatability," and wore T-shirts to rallies with chauvinistic slogans such as "Hillary: Couldn't Satisfy Her Husband, Can't Satisfy Us." Some were even spotted approvingly accompanying men whose shirts proclaimed, "She's a Cunt, Vote for Trump."

Pro-Trump/anti-Clinton merchandise, including a "Spank Me" poster, being sold outside a campaign rally in Ocala, Florida, October 2016. (Photograph by Simone Perez)

Man wearing "I Wish Hillary Had Married OJ" T-shirt, Trump campaign rally, Colorado Springs, Colorado, October 2016. (Photograph by Simone Perez)

Woman outside a Trump campaign rally, Green Bay, Wisconsin, October 2016. (Photograph by Simone Perez)

And while 54 percent of women overall voted for Clinton, compared to 39 percent for Trump, a majority of white women voted against Clinton. Presumably the Clinton haters did not see themselves partaking of misogyny and would scoff at the idea, but by our definition a vast number unquestionably consumed, spread, and exulted in it.

In the end, 47 percent of white women voted for Trump against Clinton, as did 62 percent of white men. All other demographics favored Clinton: 81 percent of Black men voted for her, as did 65 percent of Latino men, 67 percent of Latino women, and a whopping 98 percent of Black women.[39] Among conservative evangelicals, the difference was stark: 77 percent of white evangelicals who voted cast their ballot for Trump, compared to only

Man wearing crude pro-Trump/anti-Hillary T-shirt inside a Trump campaign rally, October 2016. (Photograph by Sally Kohn)

16 percent for Clinton. A significant majority of white people, including the vast majority of conservative Christians, strenuously disliked her enough to vote for what many of them even acknowledged was a truly terrible candidate, one who embodied male chauvinist misogyny, white supremacist ideology, and anti-immigration views harking back to earlier bans. Though many claimed their Trump vote was chiefly about abortion, it seemed obvious that Democratic policies kept the abortion rate lower than Republican ones (under Obama, the abortion rate dropped to its lowest level since *Roe v. Wade*).[40] Abortion appeared to be a smokescreen for a keener enthusiasm about Trump than many wished to admit. As Manne writes, misogyny "isn't simply hateful; it imposes social costs on noncompliant women who are liable to be labeled witches, bitches, sluts, and 'feminazis,' among other things."[41]

That a number of prominent, powerful men were finally held accountable during the #MeToo movement that gained steam in fall 2017 suggested attitudes might be shifting. But cases comparable to sexual scandals that had ensnared Thomas and Clinton that occurred in recent years—Brock Turner's slap-on-the-wrist punishment for raping an unconscious woman on the Stanford campus, the ongoing indifference among Trump supporters to sexual assault allegations that continued to pile up against the president, and Brett Kavanaugh's successful Supreme Court appointment despite Christine Blasey Ford's credible accusations of sexual assault—suggested that many Americans' sympathy for affronted men and toleration for the sexual abuse of women remained high. As Jia Tolentino put it in September 2018, "We now mostly accept that lots of men have committed sexual assault, but one part of the country is saying, 'Yes, this is precisely the problem,' and the other part is saying, 'Yes, that is why it would obviously be a non-issue to have one of these men on the Supreme Court.'"[42] Or in the Oval Office. It would seem that many Americans believe and accept, as the old rationalization goes, that boys will be boys.

If there is an unbroken theme structuring this gender-laden history, it is the wrath visited upon women who have, in one way or another, dared to challenge the hierarchical social order. Anti-suffragists demeaned early women's rights activists. American Catholic hierarchs beat down on Margaret Sanger and her birth control allies. Religious Right fundamentalists slurred supporters of abortion and the ERA, as well as casualties of sexual harassment who raised public protests. In all these instances, conservative forces wedded to a status quo favoring men in positions of authority over women have punished those women who resist.

They insist that women should assent obediently to traditional gender roles and stand by their man, whatever his faults. As Tammy Wynette's 1968 single by that name put it:

> You'll have bad times, and he'll have good times,
> Doin' things that you don't understand.
> But if you love him, you'll forgive him,
> . . . .
> 'Cause after all he's just a man.[43]

Let the man mistreat his woman, perhaps cheat on or even beat her; she must forgive—*after all, he's just a man*—love, and stand by him no matter what. This song, one of the most popular tracks in the history of American country music and the subject that triggered the early outrage against Hillary Clinton, is precisely illustrative of the dynamic of misogyny in American life.

In countless ways, visible and invisible, women are socialized from infancy into compliance with the social expectations for female personhood, which together comprise an overall posture of submission. Men are socialized as well—into the social expectations for male personhood and an overall posture of confident leadership, as well as the capacity for enforcing female submission by critiquing or otherwise punishing those girls or women who fail to comply with that ideal. In a myriad of subtle ways (and plenty that are not so subtle), women and men are rewarded or punished based on their obedience and skill level at occupying their respective roles. For many if not most, defiance or violation of the rules takes real mettle. Courage.

What is courage? Philosophers and ethicists have debated definitions, but most emphasize courage as "a disposition to confront fear (rather than being fearless)" in performing morally good action. It is, one writes, about "mastering (which is not necessarily the same as extinguishing) one's fears."[44] Courage is also about making a deliberate choice to act in a particular way; if one's action is driven by sheer emotion such as rage and not by measured thought, it doesn't count as courageous (at least to the philosophers). Slavoj Žižek, a Slovenian philosopher, makes an important point when he notes that our historical moment is one in which "even the most pessimistic diagnosis as a rule finishes with an uplifting hint at some version of the proverbial light at the end of the tunnel." Courage does it differently, Žižek believes: "The true courage is not to imagine an alternative, but to accept the consequences of the fact that there is no clearly discernible alternative: the dream of an alternative is a sign of theoretical cowardice, functioning as a fetish that prevents us from thinking through to the end the deadlock of our predicament. In short, the true courage is to admit that the light at the end of the tunnel is probably the headlight of another train approaching us from the opposite direction."[45] Perhaps courage need be neither optimistic nor pessimistic but humbly and knowingly unknowing about the outcome. Some people may not need hope in order to have courage, but many surely do.

After a lifetime of compliance (however long or short that lifetime thus far may be), it will take some people a good deal of courage to stand up to misogyny and resist. Refusing to give in to the policing mechanisms or to utilize them oneself as weapons against others is the principal task: Remember the cost of mocking women for their looks, weight, or apparel. Consider the absurdity of disparaging a woman's voice as raspy, her appearance as unattractively masculine, her demeanor in the world as incompetent or unlikeable. Think of the potential damage before laughing at sexist jokes or judging a woman's sexual choices. These may sound like small things, but in fact for so many of us, they are the stuff of everyday life. Simply choosing to refrain from such foolish cruelties, and speaking frankly to those who indulge them, could stoke a revolution against misogyny. And even if you believe the revolution will never come, demonstrating the courage to resist misogyny in the treatment of others as well as oneself does critically important work in the world and may *en*courage others to do the same.

4

CONVERSATION

Abortion and
Religious Liberty

Freedom lies across the field of the difficult
conversation. And the more difficult the conversation, the greater the freedom.

—Shonda Rimes, *Year of Yes*

OUR FOCUS TO NOW has been on the forthright facing of history: American slavery, buttressed by justificatory dogmas of
white supremacy that have had an untold impact on U.S. culture
and structure our politics today; immigration conflicts, in which
American citizens have persistently quarreled over policies of
entry, asylum, and patriation, arguing over the traits needed to
make "an American"; and misogyny, a perpetual force in American life upheld by women no less than men but that once more
makes a mockery of what citizens say they value. Here we shift
lenses to consider in greater detail a current controversy—over
abortion—that has important relations to each of these areas and

some lengthy historical context that is not usually included in the debate.

While the previous chapter touched briefly on the history of abortion politics, here I want to consider the subject in its more practical dimensions. This chapter will return briefly to the histories of slavery, immigration, and misogyny to think about their role in crafting the terms of the debate as it has taken shape in American life and politics. It also considers the ways in which the key values noted thus far—truthfulness, empathy, and courage—can guide us today. And it offers a fourth that might simply be termed conversation, a willing exchange across differing views that is tempered by reciprocity and moderation. "Conversation" is not typically thought of as a value; and yet a persistent truism in our time is the belief that Americans increasingly lack the skills to communicate across deepening ideological divides; many also argue that technologies of the internet and social media platforms have drastically reduced the means and incentives for genuine conversation. By invoking conversation, I do not mean to invoke a naïve wish of "can't we all just get along?," much less a false "both-sides-ism" such as media outlets trying to appeal to broad audiences sometimes employ when they give more credence to one side of a debate than the evidence would warrant—say, a piece suggesting that evolution is a mere conjecture no more demonstrable than intelligent design or that climate change is as likely to have come from natural causes as from human activity.[1] Conversations with frauds and liars are unfairly rigged and ultimately destructive. Instead, I start from the modest and observable fact that in an arena such as reproductive rights and abortion, people of conscience genuinely hold moral positions on very different sides; and yet there is far more caricaturing and condemning of the other side than there is deep conversing with persons who hold different views. Better modes of conversation about the val-

Pro-life and pro-choice demonstrators before the Supreme Court during the March for Life in Washington, D.C., January 27, 2017. (Jim Watson/ Getty/AFP)

ues we hold, including those we share and those we may not, must be sought if our politics is ever to move forward from this conflict.

Given the highly fraught nature of this subject and the fact that it involves life-and-death questions, readers ought to know where I stand on abortion. I do not judge abortion to be murder; the idea that a zygote is as naturally precious as you, reader, is a theological proposition that I do not accept. Around the midpoint of the second trimester I grow more uneasy about abortion and believe some moral questions (such as regards fetal pain) merit real scrutiny, but I think there are various circumstances during that time and even later where it can be the best choice. Women have written heart-wrenching accounts of aborting a much-wanted pregnancy at a very late stage in cases of severe fetal deformity, and I consider it just that they should have that right. And I strongly believe women's ability to control their reproductive capacity is a vital social good, a benefit to individual women and families as well as to society in the aggregate because this ability enables women's ambitions and skills to flourish—including any aspirations to parenthood they may hold—far more than when motherhood is forced upon them. Hence I favor liberal abortion laws and believe women should be authorized to make their own choices.

At the same time, I understand abortion to be a complicated issue, irreducible to the usual slogans. I sympathize with the anguish felt by those who in good faith truly believe abortion to be murder (although I question whether that is the true motive of all anti-abortion activists); as it happens, I believe that capital punishment is murder and that eating meat is ethically wrong, and I object to others treating those beliefs with intolerance or disdain. So I willingly support setting policies that would help reduce the rate of unintended pregnancies and therefore abortions, as well as policies that would better support pregnant women who choose to continue their pregnancies under difficult circumstances—and policies that would better support them as they become mothers. I would like abortion opponents to willingly fight for better benefits for poor women and children, and higher taxes if necessary to pay for them; if more of them did so, then I would feel more amenable to compromises such as greater abortion restrictions in the second half of pregnancy. To be clear, that would be a concession on my part; but I do not think such restrictions constitute an evil that would necessarily outweigh the potential goods of such a settlement. And I am realistic about the fact that concessions need to be made on all sides if abortion policy is ever to be settled in the United States. I imagine sitting in a room with people across the abortion spectrum—including some whom I write about in this chapter—and hammering out policies on abortion that we could all live with, compromises, blemishes, and all.

Because abortion is such a personal matter, I will, just for a moment, speak personally. I have knowingly been pregnant five times. Three pregnancies resulted in joyous births to the children I have loved and parented for over twenty years, Zachary, Ella, and Jasper. One pregnancy ended in a devastating miscarriage that wiped me out emotionally for several months. And one pregnancy ended with my choice to have an abortion, a situation that I grieved deeply because of its specific circumstances but a decision I never felt guilty about or regretted. In my life, the abortion has been a weightier medical procedure than other procedures that have taken about the same amount of time—extraction of my wisdom teeth, foot surgery, a routine colonoscopy—and I will always wish the pregnancy hadn't happened in the first place, so that I could have avoided the sadness and sense of loss I felt in ending it. But the abortion was not a shameful experience nor one from which I need absolution, and I'm enduringly grateful that the option was accessible to me.

Abortion, it isn't said nearly often enough, is a singular experience for each person who has one, in large part because of how strongly we are individually conditioned to feel about it by religion and other social and cultural influences. It seems to me that the fear of telling the wrong person and getting an adverse reaction keeps most women silent about any personal experiences with abortion, a silence that (needless to say) has enormous political consequences. I believe it's important not to judge others for their reproductive choices or the emotions that do or don't accompany abortion; unfortunately, the dreadful condition of abortion debate in the United States is the result of ceaseless judgment and vilification in this area going back more than half a century.

If the pollsters and other researchers are right, more often than not those favoring safe abortion access and those opposing it likewise hold views that are less rigidly fixed than can be captured by simple terms like "pro-life" or "pro-choice." Most data suggest that Americans occupy many positions along the spectrum of views. This does not mean people are namby-pamby or indifferent when it comes to abortion: they stand on ethical precepts, they have conscience claims, and they cite constitutional rights that are deemed valid in our legal structure; yet they come out all over the place in terms of their outlooks. So how do we decide this fraught issue? Does one side's moral principles win out completely over the other's, or are there ways to adjudicate fairly between them? What principles can guide us when a fundamental assertion of a sizable minority of the U.S. population—that all abortion is murder—is profoundly grave yet neither empirically verifiable nor ethically certain, and is not shared by the majority?

The subject of abortion comes under the umbrella of a broader array of issues termed reproductive rights; and this set of topics has a long and charged history, even limiting the purview to the American story. Chronicling it reminds us how little control most women have historically had over their capacity to reproduce children. Throughout the history of slavery, despite the ideology of white supremacy developed to justify the institution and the obstinate belief among whites that Blacks were their inferiors, sex and reproduction regularly occurred across the so-called color line. But not just any sex, and not just any reproduction: white enslavers not infrequently raped their enslaved women and forced them to bear any resulting children. The power relations structuring their lives meant that enslaved women had virtually no control over their reproductive capacities. All of this took place despite the fact that there were laws prohibiting sex and marriage between the races in America that went back to the 1660s, when colonial authorities banned interracial sex in an effort to promote racial hierarchies and protect the white "race" from being tainted by Black people. By 1705, the government of Virginia punished white people with prison and large fines if they were caught having sexual relations with nonwhites; ministers were also forbidden from performing interracial marriages. All the southern colonies and, later, at least forty-one states enacted antimiscegenation laws at some time during their history.

But these laws tended to be unequally applied and were rarely enforced against white men who had sex with Black women, coercively or not. So many mixed-race babies were born to enslaved women that colonial governments passed laws to force those children into slavery as well: white enslavers could actually enlarge their wealth by raping and impregnating the women they enslaved (while white women bearing mixed-race infants received harsh punishments). Black women were left wholly unprotected from rape and violent abuse, a reality that lasted long past the end of the Civil War in 1865.

Immigrant women often faced other horrors pertaining to their reproductive capacities. During the twentieth century, more than thirty states passed eugenic sterilization laws, seeking to hold down the growth of particular groups that were deemed unfit, even as eugenicists tried to boost reproduction among those considered fit. "Fit" and "unfit" designations aligned with prejudicial attitudes toward certain racial groups, social classes, and persons with a variety of physical and mental disabilities; indeed, although data have been scattered, it is estimated that more than sixty thousand disabled persons were sterilized.[2] Many sterilization laws applied to public institutions that housed the so-called feebleminded as well as the insane and epileptic. In predominantly white states, such as Indiana—which carried out roughly 2,500 compulsory sterilizations between 1907 and 1974—eugenic sterilization programs tended to target the poor, while in other states this prejudice was accompanied by racial bias against nonwhite and immigrant populations, including African Americans, Puerto Ricans, and Mexicans.[3]

California, for instance, enacted a sterilization law in 1909, and the law remained in effect until it was repealed in 1979 (a date that might strike some as uncomfortably close). Under it, those designated as morons or feebleminded could be subjected to sterilization without their consent. Around twenty thousand persons were sterilized under this law during those seven decades, making California the nation's "most zealous sterilizer" (that twenty thousand was out of a total of sixty thousand in thirty-two states). Large proportions of these persons were deemed mentally ill and/or "mentally deficient."[4] California's law targeted Mexican American women at highly disproportionate rates, coding their offspring as "delinquent, socially deviant, and more prone to feeblemindedness than 'American children.'"[5] White elites stereotyped Mexican American women as promiscuous and excessively fertile, as well as illiterate and diseased: as one American author belittlingly put it, Mexican women reproduced "countless numbers of American citizens . . . with the reckless prodigality of rabbits," a situation that would cause the "mongrelization of America."[6] The nativism propounding the idea that immigrants from Asia, eastern Europe, and Mexico were social burdens, thickly populated with criminals and the sexually deviant, mixed with eugenic prejudices against those deemed "defective" in some way, with appalling consequences for large numbers of immigrant women. In the case of California, the law required neither patient nor guardian consent for sterilizations, and there were no mechanisms for appeal. As the historians of eugenics Natalie Lira and Alexandra Minna Stern write, "Patients and relatives essentially were powerless to prevent sterilization if the medical superintendent decided the operation should be done."[7]

Finally, the long history of structural misogyny in the United States bears directly on reproductive rights. The laws of coverture meant that women had no real ownership of their bodies: they were considered the property, first, of their fathers and later, of their husbands. There was no legal concept of marital rape or consent, so men had full say about when women had sex. And without access to birth control, women had virtually no way to avoid multiple pregnancies over their lifetime, unless they resorted to hazardous attempts at abortion.

Since the early twentieth century, political struggles between progressives and conservatives have often centered on reproductive rights, from access to basic information about birth control to laws governing maternity leave and job security for pregnant women and mothers. Religiously motivated activists from Anthony Comstock to Phyllis Schlafly worked to prevent women from accessing information about sex and reproduction, strongly censuring the graphically informative reports on American men and women's sexual behavior published by the biologist Alfred Kinsey in the late 1940s and early 1950s, for instance, and then fighting against sex education in the schools during the 1960s and following decades. In the latter instance, school boards that wanted their female as well as male students to gain a better understanding of their own bodies and the biology of reproduction were shouted down by angry parents, and many public-school systems went back and forth on this issue for years, even through the abstinence-only programs that were promoted in the early 2000s by President George W. Bush.

Adding to these debates over sex education was an abortion debate thrown into turmoil by the suddenness of 1973's *Roe v. Wade* decision, which instantly decriminalized abortion across the country. Since prior to that decision most Americans, including a majority of American Catholic laypeople, had supported some measure of abortion reform that would loosen the laws prohibiting it in nearly all cases, the initial reaction was fairly calm, even positive. Southern Baptist leaders praised the *Roe* decision in its immediate aftermath. But by the mid-1980s they and other conservative Protestants had dramatically reversed course and adopted the official Catholic view—completely new to most Protestants—that abortion was murder from the instant the egg and sperm joined in the womb. That the conservative Protestant position was Catholicized in this way went almost unremarked at the time, until to many it came to seem simply obvious that Christians writ large must oppose abortion. Liberal and progressive Protestants and Catholics had long supported abortion rights for the sake of poor women who so often risked death to procure illegal abortions, and they became closer allies of pro-choice organizations such as Planned Parenthood.

Throughout its duration, the political war over abortion has been marked by the perception that the pro-life and pro-choice sides are arguing on wholly different terms, except in the paradoxical sense that each describes itself as protecting a vulnerable population from an intolerant faction of oppressors. Critics of abortion have claimed to be protecting the most vulnerable life on earth: in their eyes, these are unborn persons, fully human from the very earliest stage of pregnancy but unable to defend themselves; and believed capable, even as embryos, of severe distress and pain. Supporters of abortion rights have focused their protection claims on women, vulnerable to sexual coercion, violence, and countless modes of gender-based discrimination; and believed to have the full right to abort an embryo/fetus (not considered a "person" until some late stage in pregnancy, or even birth itself) whatever the circumstances that led to conception. Leaders and adherents of both movements claim to care deeply about the lives of both women and children, but their opponents often see them as fanatical, power-hungry charlatans.

An important theme that has pervaded the debate over abortion, like so many other debates over sexuality, is religious liberty. Religious conservatives have repeatedly claimed to perceive injury to their own religious rights or religious freedom produced by gains in gender and sexual rights of which they disapprove. The argument hasn't always worked as well for religious liberals and progressives, but they too have invoked religious liberty claims against gains on the other side. These debates have indelibly shaped a public discourse that now practically assumes that Americans—all of us—must take sides in the fight between gender/sexuality rights and religious rights. As the feminist theologian Kathleen Sands writes in her aptly titled book *America's Religious Wars: The Embattled Heart of Our Public Life:* "From the beginning, every American conflict about religious liberty has been a conflict about equality—about what counts as a 'religion,' who counts as a citizen, and how freedom can be safeguarded for all."[8]

The University of Virginia legal scholar Douglas Laycock, one of the nation's foremost experts on religious liberty and also a supporter of same-sex rights, has lamented that religious and sexual rights are so often pitted against each other. In a volume exploring the debates over religious liberty and same-sex marriage, he writes about the core conflict, which applies equally well to the abortion debate: in his analysis, it is rare for people to support the equal liberty of both conservative religious groups and sexuality activists calling for their rights. "Too many Americans continue to commit modern versions of the Puritan mistake," he remarks.

> The Puritans came to Massachusetts for religious liberty, but only for themselves. So far as they were concerned, adherents of other faiths had the liberty to go anywhere in the world outside Massachusetts, and that was quite enough religious liberty for them. Contemporary Americans are not so flagrant about protecting only themselves, but they have a similar tendency to protect only those they can sympathize with. Too many Americans react to claims of religious or sexual liberty on the basis of what they

think of the religious belief or sexual practice at issue. The appeal of liberty as such is often insufficient to override antipathy to the beliefs or practices of the group asserting its right to liberty.

A certain selfish self-interest is at work here, Laycock observes: "When the competing claims are to religious liberty and sexual liberty, people feel even more free to protect only the liberty they rely on for themselves." He goes on to note that the Constitution does not force a choice between these two liberties, and yet many people's preferences push them to act as if they do. "Religious conservatives," says Laycock, tend to argue that "sexual liberty is nowhere mentioned in the Constitution." Progressive advocates, "unable to deny that the Constitution protects the free exercise of religion, . . . construe that protection down to the vanishing point. . . . Few politicians on either left or right do any better."[9] Defending liberty on one's own side and opposing liberty for one's opponents seem to go hand in hand.

Partisans in the fight might dispute this characterization and defend themselves as caring about both sets of rights. But there's no doubting the fact that, on a whole range of issues, religious liberty groups and sexual justice or reproductive rights groups stand in opposition to one another, one side clearly perceiving the other as a unique threat. Rather than seeing potential allies in one another or approaching one another in good faith and humility, each set of activists sees the other as the chief enemy; and because they act like enemies, they are constantly proving one another's "worst fears." Laycock laments that, like so much else in politics, the "fundraising advantage" goes to those who make the most extreme arguments and stoke the greatest fear, "so that agitating the conflict is encouraged and reasoned discourse is discouraged." Most maddening of all perhaps, to Laycock, neither side sees any room for compromise but seeks to impose its own views on everyone else. On both sides, in his words, "Claims to liberty . . .

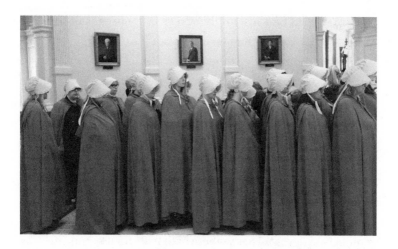

Activists dressed as subjugated women from *The Handmaid's Tale* protest an anti-abortion bill (requiring the burial of aborted fetal remains) in the Texas Capitol Rotunda, May 23, 2017. (AP Photo/Eric Gay)

would be more credible, and quite possibly more persuasive, if they did not devote so much of their energy to restricting the liberty of others."[10]

When it comes to abortion, we remain as deep in the throes of conflict as we have since 1973—deeper than 1973, in fact, since at that time the pro-life movement was small and almost entirely populated by conservative Catholics; most of the rest of the population were supporters of reform of abortion laws and greater access to abortion. Since then, much has changed. Over the decades, the costs of this conflict have been staggeringly high financially, and very, very grim. Already many abortion providers have had their lives and livelihoods threatened and even been murdered; already countless numbers of women have been harassed, sometimes viciously, on their way to exercise their legal right to a legal abortion. To those who believe that life itself begins at conception with the creation of a sacred being instantly as precious as any human living outside the womb and that abortion is murder from that instant, hundreds of thousands of lives are lost each year to abortion. One does not have to agree with this view of abortion in order to recognize the deep distress it causes people who genuinely believe it. To those who believe that grave injury is done to women who are compelled to carry unwanted pregnancies to full term, and who believe that if abortion were outlawed hundreds of thousands of women would once again seek out illegal abortions from which many would be harmed or killed, an incalculable number of women's lives could potentially be lost to abortion over time. One does not have to agree with this view in order to recognize the deep distress it causes people who genuinely believe it. That's where both truthfulness and empathy come in.

What would courage entail? Perhaps it means that abortion supporters agree to consider as good a reduction in the abortion rate, rather than treating this as an unspeakable topic. They do, after all, want to reduce the rate of unwanted pregnancies, and presumably so do abortion opponents. Can this be done, in a collaborative effort between those who consider themselves pro-life and those who consider themselves pro-choice? And perhaps it also means that abortion opponents accept the good-faith arguments of those who do not consider abortion murder and that they focus their efforts on ensuring that they themselves are not complicit with abortion services rather than trying to outlaw those for everyone else. If only it were that simple.

As Amy Gutmann and Dennis Thompson make clear in their book *Why Deliberative Democracy?*, the morality of abortion will not be resolved through deliberation. The differences are simply too stark; in their words:

> Pro-life advocates believe the fetus to be a human being, a
> person in the generic sense of the term. Their principled basis of

opposing legalized abortion is the right of an innocent human to live. Pro-choice advocates believe the fetus to be only a potential person. Their principled basis for championing legalized abortion is a woman's freedom of choice with regard to her own body. Both sides can agree on the general . . . moral principles that innocent people have a right to live and that women have a right to freedom of choice with regard to their own bodies. But they arrive at radically different conclusions about abortion because they cannot agree on whether the fetus is a full-fledged person, whether the right to life extends to the obligation of women to realize the human potential of a dependent fetus, and whether women have freedom of choice with regard to their bodies even if the life of an innocent person is at stake.

The disagreement comes down to basic "beliefs about whether the fetus is a person."[11]

That is, like same-sex marriage and, for Catholics, contraception, the question of abortion has a deep problem at its core: to quote Laycock again, "what one side views as a grave evil, the other side views as a fundamental human right." Abortion especially is seen by its opponents as "so evil" that it's not just enough to say, "Just don't have one," as pro-choicers flippantly respond to the pro-life position; like murder, which again they believe it is, abortion's fiercest critics believe it has to be forbidden outright to all, not simply those who oppose it. And so, in the view of those who support the pro-choice position, religious conservatives are meddling into a deeply personal and private decision and inflicting their own debatable belief on everyone else: as Laycock puts it, "It is a risky step to interfere with the most intimate details of other people's lives while loudly claiming liberty for yourself."[12] While I do not share all of Laycock's views regarding religious liberty, he is correct in noting that both sides have repeatedly been guilty of such sanctimoniousness and that, "What is lacking is mutual tolerance and political will."[13] Surely, if we could develop those resources above all, we could finally make headway toward workable compromises that would provide women with safe and accessible reproductive health care without unconstitutionally violating anyone's religious liberty. And that work begins with better, respectful, and more intentional conversations across ideological lines. In other words, even if the *morality* of abortion cannot be settled through deliberation, as Gutmann and Thompson argue, having the right conversations ought to be able to help us make better progress on *policy* than we have to date. But so far, the persistent division about personhood, backed up by costly visual campaigns intended to stoke emotion rather than foster empirical argument, has stymied us over and over again.

If my overall point in this volume is to confront some aspects of the history of the United States which have been charged and difficult to face, like the legacies of slavery and Jim Crow and our long history of ambivalence toward certain types of immigrants as well as the country's long struggles with misogyny, then what needs to be faced when it comes to abortion? Abortion opponents would surely say it's the mass murders of unborn children; abortion access supporters would say the suppression of women and/ or privacy rights. But it's more than that. When it comes to very basic issues regarding sex, women's rights, gender identity, and religious liberty, the value of conscience itself appears to be at stake. In her forthcoming book *Bound by Belief: Rethinking the Liberty of Conscience in Early Modern Political Thought*, Amy Gais, a Yale-trained political theorist, writes of the evolution of the partisan "culture wars" into a war over conscience: whereas both liberals and conservatives invoke the liberty of conscience as a critical component of democratic politics, their notion of what conscience demands could hardly be more different or oppositional. A particular tension regarding liberty of conscience is whether that liberty entails only an inward freedom to believe what one deems to be true or also an outward freedom, thus protecting religiously motivated conduct such as former Kentucky county clerk Kim Davis's refusal in 2015 to issue marriage licenses to same-sex couples, select institutions' refusal to cover contraceptive services in their employee health insurance plans, or Catholic hospitals' objection to supplying patients with reproductive health referrals to non-Catholic providers. To what degree does freedom of conscience justify religious exemptions from the law, so that the conscientious objector need not be complicit in others' conduct that he/she/they deems sinful? This is the critical question at stake.[14]

These are enormous issues, and quite fascinating ones. Crucial to note is the fact that they are often made fraught by one side's suspicion, if not outright rejection, of the conscience claims of the other side. Isn't the refusal to recognize same-sex marriage simply bigotry, some say? Isn't the opposition to abortion really resistance to women's equal rights? Often, we have difficulty granting a conscience claim to an opponent whose view we dislike; that is what it means to say that "conscience" is at the center of today's culture wars. Perhaps this is the place where intervention may be possible, for to offer respect to the other's claims of conscience is a step toward compromise. And by "compromise" here, I do not mean mere concession to that whom one considers an evil, unjust enemy; far better to frame it as a democratic imperative in a pluralistic society, based on deep conversation, mutual humility, and respect across multifaceted ideological differences.

Sometimes personal stories, perhaps especially from the most extreme cases, invite the most sympathy: rape victims, for instance, are one group about whom many pro-life advocates are torn and to whom a substantial majority of Americans believe abortion should be accessible. Many legislatures have made abortion much harder to access for these victims, however. Dawn Porter's powerful documentary film *Trapped,* which analyzes abortion providers in the South—several shown to be committed Christians—as they try to work around the targeted regulation of abortion providers (TRAP laws) intended to close clinics, includes the stories of two teenage rape victims impregnated by their rapists and desperate for abortions; the barriers both girls face while reeling in the grave aftermath of traumatic sexual assaults bring home the real-life circumstances thrusting so many women into the predicament of dealing with an unwanted, unasked-for pregnancy. "No woman has ever told me that she feels it's all right to have an abortion," says one attendant from a Alabama clinic recovery room, "but they have told me that this is the only decision I can make at this time. . . . It is up to me to encourage them that this decision don't have to destroy you." Soon she is shown doing just that, assuring a young girl crying over her decision, "The same God that got you through everything else you've been through . . . He's still there," before laying hands on the girl's head and lovingly praying over her. When one in three women have an abortion in their lifetime, and the majority of congregations are women, notes Christian abortion provider Dr. Willie Parker, "there are women there all the time who have made this decision," even as preachers from the pulpit preach against abortion. "Where's the love, where's the compassion, where's the ministry to these women?" he asks. Whatever one's views of abortion, facing these real-life stories in all their complexity and potential pain is vitally important.[15]

But when it comes to abortion, scornful intolerance remains the standard default. Witness the pro-life legal scholar Robert George. George, who regularly commands five-figure speaking

Dr. Willie Parker, abortion provider, at church with his family, 2015. (Trilogy Films)

fees for public dialogues with Cornel West that call for greater civility, toleration of ideas we oppose, and love on college campuses, has frequently promoted the idea of the university as "an institution that is welcoming all points of view, providing a forum for the engagement of ideas." Using the example of ethicist Peter Singer's support of the acceptability of abortion throughout pregnancy and even infanticide, George has said: "I think it is very important that we be willing to listen to anybody who's willing to come into the university context and present reasons and arguments. In other words, do business in the currency of academic discourse, the currency of reasons and arguments even if I deeply oppose, if I abominate the position being articulated. . . . What I'm against is abuse. Hurling epithets, incivility, a grunt or a name-calling episode is not making reasons and arguments."[16] But while George criticizes those who would "simply verbally assault someone or brutalize someone," in the summer of 2019 he angrily tweeted the following at presidential candidate Pete Buttigieg, after Buttigieg condemned Christian Republicans who supported the federal government's family separation policy at the border as having "lost all claim to ever use religious language": "Agreed Mr. Mayor. And for an ambitious politician who associates himself with Christianity to say it's OK to suggest that God smiles on the division of a child into a collection of severed body parts at the hands of an abortionist, has lost all claim to be other than a hypocrite."[17] As epithets go in the abortion wars, "hypocrite" may seem mild, but to slur a pro-choice advocate as indifferent to child murder is disgraceful; after all of his officious pontificating against coarse manners, George—hurling insults like the abusive name-callers he chastises—is hoist with his own petard.

George is by no means the only pro-life advocate who seems to attribute a wholesale lack of morality to the pro-choice opposition. Thankfully, there are better examples of pro-life interlocutors conversing about abortion in good faith with persons on the other side. One example is the Catholic ethicist Charles Camosy, who has spent a great deal of time actually communicating with supporters of legal abortion to understand their concerns for women's equal rights and more. Early in his thoughtful account *Beyond the Abortion Wars,* Camosy outlines several rules for discussing abortion to which he wants to hold himself accountable even as he builds his own set of arguments against abortion: those rules are "humility," "solidarity with our conversation partners," "avoiding dismissive words and phrases that erect fences," and "leading with what we are for instead of what we are against." Having urged readers to join him in thinking and speaking about abortion "fairly, precisely, and in ways that invite fruitful and honest engagement," Camosy cites a great deal of empirical evidence to undermine the notion that there are "two sides" in the abortion debate, calling it a "lazy, false, and harmful idea." Beyond the fact that most Americans identify as moderates on abortion, many seeing themselves as both "pro-life" and "pro-choice," Camosy notes that most share a concern for the unequal burdens women face due to pregnancy and childbirth; and he argues that they ought therefore be able to form alliances to support measures guaranteeing equal pay for equal work, labor protections for women who become mothers (so that employers cannot fire or refuse to hire them), full access to maternal health care, "dramatically increased paid pregnancy leave with complete job protection," universal prekindergarten programs, affordable and accessible child care, reform of adoption procedures, and more.[18]

In a legislative proposal he calls the Mother and Prenatal Child Protection Act (MPCPA), Camosy argues for these regulations alongside the banning of abortion except in cases of rape or where it is necessary to save the life of the mother; physicians performing surgical abortions in all other circumstances would be charged with a Class A felony, while indirect abortion (via the drug RU-486, for example) would be treated as a Class B felony. While far stricter than current laws and the preference of a majority of Americans, this proposal stops short of the "pro-life" goal of banning all abortions, as Camosy recognizes, and he addresses that issue thus:

> First, let me say something directly to the Catholics who fall into this group. You may not think that the MPCPA perfectly reflects your view of abortion, but you really should support something like it nevertheless. You should support it because the church explicitly teaches that faithful Catholics may support incremental legislative change if the political realities give you a proportionately serious reason to do so. And if you don't think our current

discourse on abortion in the United States gives you such a reason, frankly, you need a dose of political reality.

Camosy goes on to say that while tides are shifting against "abortion on demand," they are "absolutely *not* turning in the direction of banning all abortion." To the contrary, he notes "overwhelming support" for women to have the choice to abort in the cases of rape as well as to save the life of the mother, noting that *"almost 70 percent of 'pro-lifers'"* support these exceptions.[19] The "ban all abortion" approach has actually helped the pro-choice side, Camosy continues, because it turns attention away from the types of abortions of which most Americans ostensibly disapprove (Camosy's "on demand" category appears to include pregnancies incurred by immoral or irresponsible sexual behavior—as defined by church doctrine, presumably—as well as abortions with the goal of self-selection or avoiding a disabled child) toward the much smaller percentage of abortions in cases of rape and danger to the mother's life.

Catholic arguments against abortion are often silent about the fact that the fundamental premise that total human personhood begins at the moment of conception—or, as one theorist describes it, that "a life form with a complete set of human DNA is fully a person"—may seem self-evident to them but is nowhere close to being universally accepted as such, whatever the Roman Catholic hierarchy may teach.[20] The British legal philosopher Kate Greasley, who favors liberal laws on abortion, writes about the "self-evident" problem, quoting a vivid passage by Roger Wertheimer that gets to the crux of it:

> He [the supporter of abortion rights] doesn't know how to
> respond to the argument [that the fetus is a person] because
> he cannot *make sense* of that premise. To him, it is not simply

false, but wildly, madly false, it is nonsense, totally unintelligible, literally unbelievable. Just look at an embryo. It is an amorphous speck of coagulated protoplasm. It has no eyes or ears, no head at all. It can't walk or talk; you can't dress it or wash it. Why, it doesn't even qualify as a Barbie doll, and yet millions of people call it a human being, just like one of us. It's as if someone were to look at an acorn and call it an oak tree, or, better, it's as though someone squirted a paint tube at a canvas and called the outcome a painting—a work of art—and people believed him. The whole thing is precisely that mad—and just that sane.

Wertheimer concludes, "The liberal is befuddled by the conservative's argument, just as Giotto would be were he to assess a Pollock production as a painting."[21]

Greasley cites Robert George as one of those who imagines his position "equally self-evident to any reasonable person assessing the facts"; but while George might suppose this view is one that "can hardly be doubted," it is, Greasley writes, "one which supporters of abortion rights think not only incorrect, but, in Wertheimer's words, 'literally unbelievable' and 'wildly, madly false.'" Consequently, the "appeal to sheer self-evidence" is, for Greasley, "symptomatic of great difficulty in marshalling arguments about prenatal personhood." Abortion opponents such as Camosy—who frequently refers to the fetus as a "prenatal child" and writes that from the perspective of biology "a sprouting acorn is *already* an oak tree"—vehemently deny that their personhood arguments sound implausible if not irrational to many people, but that's wishful thinking. It is helpful to remember how absurd the idea of zygote equal rights can sound outside of traditional Catholic (and, more recently, evangelical) assumptions.[22]

Cathleen Kaveny is the Catholic ethicist who, to my mind, has the clearest and least disparaging understanding of this fact.

Before getting to a lengthy discussion of the law as it relates to abortion, she writes, "I am acutely aware of the cogency and good faith of those who disagree" with her position; and she notes that her aim is to develop a pro-life legal framework "that does not depend upon painting all the millions of Americans who adopt a pro-choice position as unreasonable or morally corrupt."[23] Rather than trying to sway non-Catholics with theological personhood arguments, or seeking to criminalize all abortions, Kaveny advocates recognizing that questions about abortion are complicated even for those who see the unborn as having full personhood rights, because of the unique burden a fetus places on the woman whose body bears it. Kaveny's hope, ultimately, is for better conversation; as she once put it to me in an interview:

> What I would say to the pro-life side, and also to the pro-choice side is: you know, try to see why the issue is hard. What is the best situation/case you can put for the people on the other side of the issue? What do they care about that you can connect to? And then I think you get to a position where you can say, "Well, I can see how you feel that way; that really is an important issue. And it's not that I deny that's an important issue, it's just that in this case, I think the other is a more important issue."

In Kaveny's view, this approach is a much better way to have a conversation than accusing others of being "utterly opposed to, you know, the value of human life on the one hand or women's dignity and equality and autonomy on the other." Making such accusations falsifies an opponent's actual position. "I don't think trying to manipulate people is a great way of trying to convince people." A "more mutually respectful conversation" that focuses on values such as autonomy and solidarity, Kaveny concludes, is our best way forward out of our self-sabotaging polarization.[24]

"Black Children Are an Endangered Species," from the "Too Many Aborted" billboard campaign, Atlanta, 2010. (AP Photo/John Bazemore)

One of the most controversial strategies of attempted persuasion by some pro-life groups is the effort to suggest that abortion is a tool of Black genocide. Ad campaigns targeting African Americans have stressed this message, such as billboards proclaiming, "Black children are an ENDANGERED SPECIES" and "The most dangerous place for an African American is in the womb." Something of a firestorm arose over these and another set of billboards placed in Chicago's predominantly African American South and West Side neighborhoods that showed then-president Obama's profile next to the statement, "Every 21 minutes, our next possible LEADER is ABORTED."

As the legal scholar Dorothy Roberts and others have analyzed, battles over abortion rights have repeatedly centered on Black women, who are more likely than white women to have unintended pregnancies and who, according to the Centers for Disease Control and Prevention, account for roughly 38 percent of all

Anti-abortion billboard, New York, 2011. (Photograph by Mario Tama/Getty Images News)

Anti-abortion billboard, Chicago, 2011. (Photograph by Scott Olson/Getty Images News)

abortions in the United States. Black women also, writes Roberts, "are more likely to be deterred by restrictive abortion laws—and to risk injury and death as a result, both from unsafe pregnancies and unsafe abortions." The billboards above were part of large pro-life campaigns around 2010–11 that placed more than a hundred billboards in Arkansas, Atlanta, Chicago, Milwaukee, Los Angeles, Texas, and elsewhere; the campaigns falsely claimed that Planned Parenthood and its founder, Margaret Sanger, intentionally located clinics in Black neighborhoods in order to commit Black genocide. But in Roberts's analysis, the abortion-as-Black-genocide message actually "promoted . . . racist ideology" by "declaring Black women's wombs unsafe" and ignoring the poverty and other social factors that caused high rates of unplanned pregnancies in Black communities. Black women themselves, she argues, were being blamed for genocide against their own people and were treated condescendingly as "incapable of making their own reproductive decisions."[25] Another example appears in the film *Trapped*, when a white woman protesting outside a clinic angrily yells at abortion provider Willie Parker: "What sickens me is that you're a Black man, and that you're having Black women go in there and destroying Black lives! *All* Black lives matter! *All* Black lives matter! *All* lives matter!"[26] The upshot has been a conservative pro-life message tapping into progressive antiracism efforts, one that pro-choice supporters view as deceitful and racist co-optation intended to shame both Black providers and the women who seek abortions.

It's not only the pro-life side that can be choleric and condescending, of course; often enough, advocates who believe in every woman's right to a safe, legal abortion attribute motives that are deceptive, despotic, and hypocritical to the pro-life opposition without grappling with some of the basic issues (such as fetal pain or eugenic engineering) that trouble many who resist abortion. In *PRO: Reclaiming Abortion Rights*, Katha Pollitt rips into the arguments of such pro-life conservatives as Paul Ryan and Rick Santorum, as well as their fellow Catholic Robert George. She accuses George and his cowriter, Christopher Tollefsen, in their book *Embryo: A Defense of Human Life*, of pretending to speak the language of science as a cover for their true language of theology. She quotes them and intersperses her own commentary here:

> "We can know from science what the embryo is." It is "a complete, albeit developmentally immature, human being" that deserves "full moral respect." Religion has nothing to do with it. "Human-embryo ethics is, in this regard, no different from the ethics of our treatment of minorities or dependents. Human beings are capable of understanding, through reason, that it is morally wrong and unjust to discriminate against someone because he is of a different race or has a different ethnic heritage. And we are capable of understanding that it is wrong and unjust to discriminate against someone because of his age, size, state of development, location, or condition of dependency."

But it's just garbage, responds Pollitt, to suggest that abortion is discrimination against—to quote George and Tollefsen again—"a very young child." In her view, it is ludicrous—what we've seen Harry Frankfurt call *bullshit*—to equate a woman's decision to abort because she cannot afford a fifth or sixth child with vicious racism. Nonsense that may be, but the scorn fails to reckon with the heart of their argument, which is about personhood. While Pollitt identifies a pattern in which the authors first derive their position from their religion and only secondarily search for it in science, the position itself merits serious consideration and cogent response à la Greasley, not derisive dismissal.[27]

Pollitt is not alone. There is a dearth of engagement on the pro-choice side with ethical questions about personhood and the moral status of the fetus. More often, abortion supporters condemn pro-life advocates as embodying misogyny while also mocking them as stupid. This was the case when the author and pundit Molly Jong-Fast, covering the influential Conservative Political Action Conference (CPAC) in 2019, wrote a series of tweets about what she called "an extremely scary pro-life panel" with Ben Carson and other leaders, including a contemptuous line meant for laughs, "I guess Doctor Ben thinks life begins at sperm."[28] Or when, in response to an Indiana law mandating that abortion clinics must cremate or bury every aborted fetus as human remains, the comedian Sarah Silverman retorted: "Funerals for fucking aborted fetuses? I would like to speak at those funerals. [*In falsetto mock preaching voice:*] 'He lived the way he died, he died the way he lived: the size of a sesame seed with no discerning brain function.'"[29]

To supporters of abortion rights, such laws are indeed grim in the extreme, attacking women's rights and imposing a theological belief onto people who do not hold it. From this angle, conservative opposition to abortion appears part and parcel of a larger patriarchal worldview resting on men's authority over women—a belief seemingly proven by the fact that the Catholic Church and the conservative Protestant groups that most staunchly fight abortion have typically only allowed men to serve as church leaders making and enforcing all the rules by which women must abide. Such a suspicion, with its credible correlations, makes it very difficult for abortion rights advocates to sustain respect for the pro-life moral conscience claims; the preferred strategy is to find relief in biting humor among like-minded critics who feel oppressed by these regulations, an approach that has real benefits: it feels cathartic, fosters solidarity, and holds undeniable appeal to women who feel brutally subjugated by patriarchal power. Writ large, however, the contempt and loathing bred toward one's ideological opponents through everlasting condescension and nonchalance toward their ethical claims are more corrosive than constructive.[30]

Frances Kissling, former head of Catholics for Choice, is one of the few national pro-choice leaders who laments the worst of the rhetoric on the pro-choice side, along with the refusal to deal frankly with the personhood questions at stake. To her fellow abortion supporters, she writes:

> We can no longer pretend the fetus is invisible. . . . We must end the fiction that an abortion at 26 weeks is no different from one at six weeks. These are not compromises or mere strategic concessions, they are a necessary evolution. The positions we have taken up to now are inadequate for the questions of the 21st century. We know more than we knew in 1973, and our positions should reflect that. The fetus is more visible than ever before, and the abortion-rights movement needs to accept its existence and its value. . . . Very few people would argue that there is no difference between the decision to abort at 6 weeks and the decision to do so when the fetus would be viable outside of the womb, which today is generally at 24 to 26 weeks.

And yet, Kissling notes, "it is rare for mainstream movement leaders to say that publicly." Still, they must.

> Abortion is not merely a medical matter, and there is an unintended coarseness to claiming that it is. We need to firmly and clearly reject post-viability abortions except in extreme cases. . . . Those kinds of regulations are not anti-woman or unduly invasive. They rightly protect all of our interests in women's health and fetal life. Even abortions in the second trimester, especially after 20 weeks, need to be considered differently from those that happen early in pregnancy.[31]

Kissling says more in this 2011 op-ed that shows she is still far from Camosy and the opposition to abortion, but her intentional engagement with those parties is evident and makes for a much more hopeful engagement with these issues than most leaders demonstrate.

There may be a case to be made that, by not facing the profound moral qualms many pro-life people have toward abortion and taking them seriously, many in the pro-choice camp have left themselves more vulnerable to the likelihood that their own conscience claims will be disregarded and undervalued. Treat the other side's issues as a smokescreen for misogyny, and yours might be treated as camouflage for religious intolerance. Call out the opposition for hypocrisy, and the charge will come roaring back. But this is hardly a causal relation at this point; the attacks are decades old and hardly need a match to light them. The first step out of this destructive clash, surely, is listening in good faith to the other side and persuading persons on that side to converse.

If the pro-life moral claim of protecting innocent life is fairly straightforward, what of the pro-choice moral claims? Ever since the Texas-born Southern Baptist minister Howard Moody and a number of Protestant and Jewish clergy colleagues formed the Clergy Consultation Service on Abortion in 1967, liberal and progressive Christians have publicly staked their own conscience claims in favor of legal access to abortion. Moody laid these out some years later: "Very few [professionals] were willing to admit that the reasons a woman became pregnant when she preferred not to be had to do with a whole complex of problems related to unsatisfactory sex education, inadequate birth control measures, the heavy moral burden placed on single women if they performed sexually out of marriage, and most importantly related to a way in which men looked at women and put them in their place." Remembering all that women had had to go through in those days in order to secure a risky, painful, and illegal abortion, "one can only conclude that abortion was directly calculated, whether consciously or not, to be an excessive, cruel, and unnecessary punishment, physically and psychologically, of women."[32]

Moody perceived profound moral implications in the double standard that made women the victims of unintended pregnancy, even though men were just as responsible (and in cases of rape or other coercions, more so). The abortion counseling and referral service he established, along with numerous other Protestant ministers and Jewish rabbis, was aimed at women in need. Christian and Jewish clergy, deeply revered in their respective congregations and broader denominational affiliations, were serving on the side of increasing women's access to abortion, rather than working to restrict abortion rights. These religious leaders were not calling eight-week embryos "babies," nor women who terminated early pregnancies "murderers." After decades of vicious accusations, highly visible activism, and even violent killings of abortion providers by some members of conservative religious groups in recent years, it is worth remembering that religious leaders were among the pioneers on the other side of the issue as well. As one pro-choice pastor in Missouri rightly noted some time ago, "Religious opponents of choice have convinced themselves, and much of the media and the American public, that they hold the only valid religious position on abortion. They are profoundly mistaken."[33]

Whether religious or secular, advocates of access to safe and legal abortion have staked a moral claim on helping women in dire circumstances, many of them sexually exploited or abandoned and all facing a major life-altering event—the creation of a dependent person—they had not requested and did not want. As Kissling put it, "As a Catholic . . . with the notion that the poor should be our first priority . . . I'm on the side of the poor."[34] Another pro-choice Christian leader is the Reverend Traci Blackmon, associate general minister for Justice and Local Church Ministries for the United Church of Christ. She agrees that abortion is particularly an issue for poor women and that the legislators working to ban it aren't concerned about "life" so much as "control." As she put it at a 2019 rally in Missouri: "We stand with women as the inherent beneficiaries of personal autonomy and self-determination over our own bodies. We stand on the foundation of our sacred text and in the shadow of the Universal Declaration of Human Rights and declare that the violation of a woman's right to choose is an act of gender-based violence. And we will not be silent."[35]

Dr. Willie Parker, the Christian obstetrician and abortion provider featured in *Trapped*, also agrees. In his book *Life's Work: A Moral Argument for Choice*, Parker writes of giving his patients the "medical truth":

> Before twenty-two weeks, a fetus is not in any way equal to "a baby" or "a child." It cannot survive outside the uterus because it cannot breathe—not even on a respirator. It cannot form anything like thoughts. Up until twenty-nine completed gestational weeks, despite what the antis may say, the scientific consensus is that it cannot feel anything like pain. I tell women that having this abortion now will not impede their future ability to have children—as many as they want—as long as their fertility persists. I do not engage in or perpetuate any of the culture's sentimental notions about the primacy of motherhood in women's lives; I regard the meeting of sperm and egg as a biological event, no less miraculous but morally and qualitatively different from a living, breathing, human life, imbued with sacredness only when the mother, or the parents, deem it so.

Parker writes of feeling infuriated "that the antis have shrouded their case in the language of God" and "seized the moral high ground," while the pro-choice side has "never mounted a signifi-cant religious or moral counterargument."[36]

In his book, Parker aims to do just that, debunking the claim that all Christian doctrine teaches that life begins at conception and using science to discredit, at great length, "the ridiculous claim that abortion is murder" since "life is a process"—"a galaxy of contingent, interconnected conditions that must be met in order for a single human to achieve progress, maturation, and fulfillment"—and "not a switch that turns on in an instant, like an electric light." He also cites scripture to point out that throughout the Hebrew bible, "the death of a fetus is regarded as a loss but not a capital crime" and "a fetus becomes human when—and only when—its head emerges from the birth canal." Ultimately, he writes, "this recasting of fetuses as babies—tiny people who feel pain and are in need of society's protection—amounts to nothing more than a cynical marketing campaign," not an unassailable Christian truth.[37]

Other Christian arguments favoring abortion rights are more restricted: Kira Schlesinger, an Episcopal priest, argues that since we cannot know exactly when an embryo becomes a person, we should trust women to make conscientious choices for themselves; but she is at pains to add that this "does not mean that we celebrate the decision to terminate a pregnancy." To the contrary, "We can still hold that abortion is a tragedy, a loss, even a death of sorts, and do everything in our power to work toward a world in which women are less inclined to make that choice."[38] Parker criticizes this type of "third way" talk that, in a naïve attempt to build "common ground" with pro-lifers, uses language casting "abortion as morally difficult and the women who sought them as agonized, fretful, and full of pain." But Schlesinger wants Christians to "acknowledge the tragic element present in any abortion," even while supporting a woman's freedom of conscience in making the decision whether to abort. Analyzing the anti-abortion arguments of Camosy and others, Schlesinger finds that they do not take into account the realities of our society and concludes, "The most dangerous policies for women and children are those that limit or prohibit abortion access without having measures in place that support families and children. We cannot ban abortion and cut free school lunch."[39]

These Christian arguments favoring abortion rights come down to the view that a woman's life and well-being trump any rights or interests attributed to the embryo, at least through the first twenty weeks. Whether seeing an element of tragedy in all or just some abortions—the pro-choice Christian writers cited here seem united in seeing late-term abortion as tragic, even if necessary—writers and thinkers such as Kissling, Blackmon, Parker, and Schlesinger wholly trust women to make their own personal choices. These leaders also hold a shared conviction that many of those seeking to ban abortion ultimately care far more about enforcing their own systems of morality upon women than about supporting their well-being or that of the fetus they may carry; and some clearly see hypocrisy in the inconsistent "pro-life" position that apparently favors saving embryos over fighting the death penalty or supporting policies that better help the poor. But some, at least, still care about trying to converse with those who, like Kaveny, hold genuine moral doubts about abortion yet are also committed to possibilities for negotiation and compromise.

As to the charge of hypocrisy against abortion opponents, I am inclined to try to see it differently, at least when it comes to the rank-and-file (as opposed to calculating politicos who wield abortion as a weapon). Most if not all of us hold inconsistent positions on many issues, and this fact seems not inherently hypocritical. More strategically, calling someone a hypocrite is not a recipe for changing that person's mind; it's more of a declaration of surrender via insult that the other is either too evil or too stupid to acknowledge the truth. The charge can certainly be true in nefarious circumstances and among crooks and liars who may be all around us. But to indict all of one's abortion rivals as hypocrites shows only one's own lack of imagination, insight, or integrity.

Where does this leave us? On the one hand, for some people conversation is pointless. Under the rigidly set terms of the current debate, after all, there is little possibility for a satisfying compromise with abortion: a fetus either is or is not a full-fledged person, and either abortion is murder from conception or it is not. On the other hand, there is clearly room for far more illuminating conversations that could help us progress toward a much better political debate about abortion than we have now. We could talk more about social policies that reduce the occurrence of unplanned pregnancies and thereby lower the abortion rate. We could discuss the difference most people apparently perceive (according to social science researchers) between the termination of a newly conceived zygote, a six-week-old embryo, and a seven-month-old fetus. After all, many of us who have had abortions were already mothers or became mothers later in our lives: we have borne infants into the world; we are experienced at feeling the somatic differences and changes that occur during pregnancy and the joy of bringing new life into the world and falling in love with our tiny newborns; we are not cold toward young life or apathetic toward children. Those of us who have not had abortions, or who could not think of having an abortion under any but the most extreme circumstance, could ask more questions and render fewer judgments on those in different life circumstances. Those of us who have undergone miscarriages could help make others aware of the sorrow that can accompany the end of a pregnancy, whether planned or unplanned. In short, whatever our life experience, we could try to have better conversations about sex and sexuality and the vast array of reasons why women daily find themselves desiring an abortion. And all of these conversations will need to be grounded in the values laid out in the earlier chapters of this book: truthfulness, empathy, and courage.

First, truthfulness: Without accusing either the pro-life or the pro-choice movements writ large with untruthfulness, both movements, through their sloganeering and other practices, have repeatedly used disingenuous arguments to make their positions sound simple and obvious and the views of their opponents stupid and evil. Abortion opponents have attempted to scare women away from abortions by claiming falsely that they're linked to breast cancer or infertility; or to sicken them with greatly exaggerated, gruesome accounts of late-stage or "partial birth" abortion. Abortion supporters have discounted the emotions that surround some women when they decide to have an abortion, treating these feelings as something shameful if not abnormal and making it seem as if normal women experience abortion no differently than the removal of a wart in the dermatologist's office. A commitment to truthfulness in this debate won't come easily after all these years, but it would certainly be a good start.

And secondly, empathy: What would happen if pro-choice and pro-life advocates worked hard to imagine the moral case on the other side of the issue? What if pro-choice advocates would agree to a discussion about the moral status of the fetus at different stages of gestation, and pro-lifers would agree to talk about the realities of grinding poverty, misogyny, and the consequences of rape in our society, as well as the impact on women across economic classes of raising babies before they have financially stable adult lives? What if conversation participants committed themselves to that classic marriage-counseling technique of mirroring the message of one's partner and expressing it without judgment in that person's own terms? What if people on all sides of this debate, and across the spectrum in the middle range, pledged to address others' positions *as they really are,* rather than some grotesque or ridiculous caricature like "antiwoman" or "baby killer," "fanatical bigot" or "abortion Nazis"? And what if advocates on each side stopped treating as traitors or sellouts those who mostly share their values and perspective but may have some dissenting views—the pro-lifer who could accept drug-induced abortions of early embryos, or the pro-choicer who rejects postviability abortions except in very rare cases—or hold misgivings about the messaging and the lack of moderation on their side?

Finally, courage: Insisting upon truthfulness and empathy in one's own dealings with abortion and holding others accountable too will depend on courage. So too will taking the risk of alienating some influential and powerful spokespeople in one's own general camp who may take any sign of compromise as weakness and defeat. And so too will recognizing that all of these efforts may fail, at least at the macro-level of state and federal policy. Perhaps the closest American partisans on abortion can come to compromise is obligating ourselves to converse thoroughly, seek ways to empathize with those who hold opposing views, and continue the effort no matter what.

CONCLUSION

Small Promptings for
Making the World Over

We made the world we're living in and we have to make
it over.

—James Baldwin, "Notes for a Hypothetical Novel: An Address"

IT'S NO SECRET THAT countless numbers of Americans living in
the early twenty-first century have experienced anxiety, anger,
and feelings of helplessness about the state of the United States—
its political polarization, social institutions, religious and cultural
divides, and much else. Years of public speaking about religion
and U.S. politics have persistently reminded me of that. Again
and again, in Q&A periods after lectures, audience members have
raised some version of the question, "What can we do to improve
things?" Or, "What can *I* do to make a difference where I am?"
These questions invariably come up in discussions at colleges
and universities, congregations, and a wide variety of civic public
spaces, as well as private conversations, small-group dialogues,
and classroom debates. I take the questioner to be asking what

practices and habits people can cultivate in order to address the systemic problems of inequality and injustice, public mistrust, and polarization that perniciously infect us as a nation. In writing these interconnected essays about truthfulness, empathy, courage, and conversation, I have tried to address some of the values I think we would all do well to be mindful of; here at the end I'd like to offer some suggestions for everyday life.

Frankly I have often stumbled when trying to offer answers to the "what can we do?" question, because the commonplace answers seem so crudely simplistic: "Try to meet more people who hold different views than you do." "Host a dinner party with both liberals and conservatives centered on discussing a hard topic such as racism." "Go out into communities that aren't your own and try to listen and understand people there." All of these activities are important and might be effective in some settings—indeed, we would arguably all be better off if we did more of this type of mixing and did our best not to simply cluster among those like us—but they're also obvious and trite, just a bit too on the nose.[1] Can mutual understanding and common ground be found in today's controversies, through principled efforts made by parties on all sides? What practices will work to foster such deep conversation, mutual humility, and respect?

My conviction, readers know well by now, is that these practices begin with the forthright facing of history such as I've tried to lay out in these essays. Chapter 1 elaborated the legacies of slavery that so deeply haunt the United States but that, as W. E. B. Du Bois and many other critics have shown, have received far less attention in classrooms than they should. I considered the imperative to confront our nation's brutal legacy of slavery and white supremacist ideology, to reject the ignorance—white ignorance—that has sheltered white innocence and prevented even people of apparent goodwill who would like to work against racism from grasping anything close to the full picture. That led to the value of *truthfulness,* a practice of seeking fuller and fairer accounts, asking why our current accounts need revision (and what forces led to errors and exclusions), and what changes we need to make to help different parts of our history be heard, known, and understood. As I tried to suggest, truthfulness as a rigorous project of history-telling is a value that I believe we need to be discussing and working to cultivate as part of the necessary work of strengthening the best parts of our democracy and extending its promises more systematically to all people within our borders. And so any practical tools we come up with here will have to have truthfulness as a necessary foundation. In James Loewen's words from *Lies My Teacher Told Me,* there is a "reciprocal relationship between truth about the past and justice in the present. . . . Telling the truth about the past can help us make it right from here on."[2]

Chapter 2 focused on the long history of immigration in America and the multiplicity of attitudes U.S. citizens have held toward foreigners, often desperate, wanting to migrate here. I explored the ambivalence toward specific classes of migrant people, who have heard all the language about America being a beacon of freedom to the world and who want to come and live here, with all the questions this raises of whether and how to "welcome the stranger." This led to pondering empathy as an instrument for approaching past and present ambivalence toward migrant people and the ways it might help us be more open to the desperation that has led so many people, perhaps including our own ancestors, over the years to seek freedom in countries like the United States. Our toolkit will also need a baseline of empathy in its contents, but it cannot be the weak variety that aims only at one's own kind; what we want is the sort of robust empathy that expands beyond the in-group and crosses lines of political, religious, social, and other differences.

Chapter 3 dealt with the nation's long indecision over women's rights and its return to structural gender hierarchy again and again. Misogyny as a set of enforcement mechanisms upholding structural sexism was the chief subject, and I focused on the history of misogyny from coverture laws through the crusade for and against women's suffrage, the birth control movement, second-wave feminist causes such as reproductive rights and the Equal Rights Amendment, sexual harassment cases into the #MeToo era, and Donald Trump's presidential election. The wrath-laden punishments visited upon women who have resisted the patriarchal order were visible throughout; and it is well worth pondering the courage it literally takes for many women and nonbinary people to resist the subordinate positions to which they are most often relegated, as well as for men themselves to stand up on behalf of those unequally treated and demand better.

Chapter 4 shifted to the highly fraught subject of abortion, one of the most divisive issues of our time. I tried to offer fair readings of a range of positions, most of them Christian since in the United States the chief opposition to abortion comes from some sectors of the church; I also noted examples of bad faith, inflammatory rhetoric among both those who oppose abortion rights and those who support them. Delineating these positions hardly solves the political conflicts in which subjects like abortion are caught up, but I tried to offer up some hope for reducing the viciousness and even violence that has often characterized these conflicts: along with truthfulness, empathy, and courage, I contemplated conversation—tempered by restraint, reciprocity, and moderation—as a practice that could enable better listening and even appropriate compromises where possible.

Each of these issues belongs to all of us, part of our shared life together. I've already quoted, as the epigraph to this book and again in the introduction, Danielle Allen's powerful statement, "We are all always awash in each other's lives, and for most of us that shared life, recorded as history, will be the only artifact we leave behind." I was privileged to be invited to participate with Allen, Stephen Heintz, and Eric Liu in the American Academy of Arts and Sciences' Commission on the Practice of Democratic Citizenship, which resulted in a final report, published in 2020, titled *Our Common Purpose: Reinventing American Democracy for the 21st Century*. That report contains a set of recommendations for structural, institutional, and individual ways to improve our current political system and the climate of polarization that has had such noxious effects on our polity. To readers of the current volume, I could not recommend that report more enthusiastically and encourage readers to consult it for a plethora of good ideas that very much serve to make the world over in tangible, concrete ways.[3]

Part of what we can all do daily is to practice the values that we know are critically important for our collective life together, including the values of truthfulness, empathy, courage, and conversation. As I hope my analysis has made clear, I am not advocating these values on religious grounds—none of them is owned by any religious tradition or by "religion" more generally—but for the pragmatic, strategic reason that we need them to live peaceably together. For decades, the nation's culture has been battered by forces that directly oppose these values: in politics and in other social arenas, events have been driven not by truthfulness but by willful deceit, not by empathy but by indifference to the needs of others, not by courage but by fearful cowardice, and not by conversation but by unyielding refusal to listen to or engage charitably with others. All of these factors have, in tangible ways, made the world worse.

Holding ourselves accountable for our personal practice of these values is important, but it is not enough. We must be willing to hold others accountable too, from our fellow citizens up through our leaders at every level. In writing about accountability, ethicists emphasize the importance of reciprocal relationships among ordinary citizens. Accountability is particularly important in democratic societies, in which citizens hold not only one another to account but their authorities as well. Governments cannot simply go to war or torture people or jail their own citizens without explanation; if they did, their power would be unaccountable and might be declared illegitimate (although the example of President Trump successfully getting away with much that previous presidents have not suggests a crisis in our means of calling government to account). In any event, just as we must hold our leaders accountable, so too must we hold one another accountable for our established norms so that we will be, in one ethicist's words, "in a position to build coalitions and forge solidarity across difference."[4]

Can our fractured nation make peace? We live in a tough moment to be asking that question, but there have been many tough moments before. In some ways, my greatest concern about the possibilities for peace is whether the portion of the nation that seems to have been utterly swindled by the "fake news" that has grown like a kudzu invasion over large swaths of our country can come to face that truth, and what it would take to be able to shift in a different direction when they truly believe that credible news sources such as mainstream newspapers and network news programs (not to mention government entities) are constantly spewing lies. How we listen to one another, how we diminish the fear that has driven so much of our polarization, and how we restore the commitment to stand united, hold one another accountable, and collaborate with one another across ordinary political divides is the great social question of our time. Perhaps the Biden-Harris era offers us, all of us, a new beginning.

Nearly thirty-five years after publishing *The Handmaid's Tale,* Margaret Atwood's sequel, *The Testaments,* appeared, to enormous acclaim. While the patriarchal violence and grim despair of Gilead persist, the second novel focuses on three women who successfully defy the regime, at first quietly and then quite explosively, and so offers a modicum of hope. Two of them are the daughters of the original narrator of *Handmaid,* Offred; while in a stunningly delicious twist the third is Aunt Lydia, the most fearsome and sadistic of the female enforcers in the original tale. Their motives for working to destroy Gilead differ, but they all center on the terrible corruption and deceitfulness embodied by the supposedly godly ruling class. That these women, eventually collaborating together, expose and essentially annihilate the patriarchal order of Gilead provides a more-than-satisfying ending for twenty-first-century Atwood fans, who are reminded that ordinary people can and do make a difference. As Michiko Kakutani, in her review of *The Testaments,* puts it: "Agency and strength, Atwood seems to be suggesting, do not require a heroine with the visionary gifts of Joan of Arc, or the ninja skills of a Katniss Everdeen or Lisbeth Salander—there are other ways of defying tyranny, participating in the resistance or helping ensure the truth of the historical record."[5] In an era that some have characterized as an age of helplessness and hopelessness, we need stories that remind us our actions can and do count and that we can, indeed, make the world over.

As Baldwin said, so many years ago, we—by "we" he was speaking specifically of writers, and I would add scholars, but he really meant *all of us*—must start by telling as much of the truth as we can bear. But we cannot stop there: instead, we must then tell a little more, and more, and more, until we realize that the atrocities of history can be faced and that, indeed, they must be if they are to be changed. This task of bearing the truth is an urgent and fundamental challenge on which other urgent actions to make over our world must stand. Confronting our hatreds and the underlying fears that drive them—white fear of enslaved Africans and their free descendants, American fear of foreign immigrants, fear of women's freedom and the upending of gender hierarchy, fear of engaging other viewpoints on complex questions such as abortion—can move us along, at least to some degree. Managing our fears, we can begin to shape new visions, new ideals for our lives and for the future, new worlds. And then, it's up to us to build them.

ACKNOWLEDGMENTS

This book of essays is based on the Richard E. Myers Lectures that I had the privilege of delivering at University Baptist Church in Charlottesville, Virginia, in February 2019. I am honored to have been selected for this endowed series and offer thanks to the senior minister, Dr. Matthew Tennant, as well as the anonymous benefactor of the lectures for inviting me. I am also grateful to the Myers Lectures selection committee members from the University of Virginia, particularly Larry Bouchard and Kevin Hart. Matt and his wife, Melanie; Debra Bryant and Larry Groves; and Ed and Carolyn Lowry offered gracious hospitality and conversation over meals during my week's visit. Other church and community members as well as University of Virginia faculty and students attended one or more of the lectures, and many offered cogent reflections. Matthew Hedstrom, Charles Mathewes, and Ricardo Padrón were especially thoughtful participants and interlocutors in the lectures, and I appreciate their friendship and contributions.

As a devoted UVA alumna (CLAS '89), I consider it a special privilege to have delivered these lectures in the shadow of the University, just blocks from Grounds and within view of the construction site for the long-awaited Memorial to Enslaved

Laborers. Karl Shuve kindly hosted a lunch for me with graduate and undergraduate students in Religious Studies. And I still marvel at the unexpected opportunity during my visit to attend—courtside!—the men's basketball game between UVA and Georgia Tech; that Cavalier team, coached by Tony Bennett, routed the Yellow Jackets 81–51 and went on to win, for the first time ever, the NCAA men's championship six weeks later. Thank you, Larry and Debra, and go Hoos!

Serendipitously, in the months prior to writing the lectures, I received an invitation from the American Academy of Arts and Sciences to participate in its newly formed Commission for the Practice of Democratic Citizenship, cochaired by Danielle Allen, Stephen Heintz, and Eric Liu. The Commission focused close attention on strategies for strengthening U.S. democracy through deeper citizen engagement, resulting in the 2020 report *Our Common Purpose: Reinventing American Democracy for the 21st Century*. Through my participation, I took part in numerous meetings and conversations that focused on the key values, norms, practices, and narratives emerging from the Commission's work; these discussions turned out to be quite generative for conceptualizing and drafting the lectures, deepening my own awareness about the ways that Americans learn about U.S. history and think about the meanings and paradoxes of liberty, democracy, and citizenship. I am grateful to have been invited to join the Commission and am especially indebted to Danielle both for her own inspiring work and for inviting me to draft a memo on "shared values" for the Commission, a short piece that proved foundational for my thinking in this book. Thanks too to Stephen and Eric and to staff members, especially Darshan Goux; and to my fellow Commission members for much productive debate and outstanding collaboration.

At Washington University in St. Louis, participants in the Colloquium on American Religion, Politics, and Culture at the John C. Danforth Center on Religion and Politics read early drafts of two chapters and offered excellent observations. Many thanks to Neal Aggarwal, Tazeen Ali, Fannie Bialek, Ben Davis, Valerie Elverton Dixon, Rebecca Epstein-Levy, Amy Gais, Aaron Griffith, Rachel McBride Lindsey, Dana Lloyd, Laurie Maffly-Kipp, Lerone Martin, Charlie McCrary, Cyrus O'Brien, Adam Park, Leigh Schmidt, Paul Schultz, Mark Valeri, Ismene Vedder, David Warren, and Anna Whittington, all of whom provided incisive comments and critiques that I have taken into account. Fannie offered particularly incisive and nuanced comments on "truthfulness" that greatly improved that analysis. And as both the text and endnotes clearly show, my thoughts owe a great deal to the scholarship of others—historians especially but also writers across a range of academic, professional, and literary fields.

David Hackett, a dear friend as well as comrade in the guild, invited me to present some of this work at the University of Florida; even better, he read the manuscript in full and offered highly perceptive observations and suggestions for its improvement. Eric Brandt, editor in chief at the University of Virginia Press, offered keen editorial guidance at every step. Kate Wheeling, Susan Murray, and Ellen Satrom made crucial technical as well as aesthetic improvements. The insights and suggestions of the press's two anonymous readers made this a much better, more nuanced book. Needless to say, the remaining errors and limitations are solely mine.

My greatest personal role models for living out the values discussed in these pages are my parents. I am inexpressibly fortunate that both of them embody what it means to aspire to truthfulness, empathy, courage, and genuinely mutual conversation. My mother-in-law and late father-in-law likewise have exemplified these values in the effort to live well for others. Finally, as always,

Leigh and our three children, Zach, Ella, and Jasper, are my greatest sources of joy and hope for the future. Love you forever.

Acknowledgments usually end there, but it would be wrong in the current moment to conclude without honoring the memory of those who have suffered and died in what many have called the twin pandemics of systemic racism and COVID-19 ravaging both the United States and the global community more broadly. Though the first of these has persisted over centuries while the second only recently became a scourge for humans, both are wreaking devastation today that too often feels unbearable. No words are adequate, but I hope that mine may be, in part, a memorial to each of the lost and broken souls—and a promise that we who survive, even temporarily, will honor you by making this world over.

NOTES

INTRODUCTION

1. Margaret Atwood, *The Handmaid's Tale* (New York: Anchor, 1988), 211; *The Handmaid's Tale*, "Faithful," Hulu video, 53:22, May 10, 2017, https://www.hulu.com/watch/ebae93e6-dd44-40e7-9c2f-57177a4e31f3.

2. James Baldwin, "As Much Truth as One Can Bear," *New York Times*, January 14, 1962, 1; Eddie S. Glaude Jr., *Begin Again: James Baldwin's America and Its Urgent Lessons for Our Own* (New York: Crown, 2020).

3. James Baldwin, "Notes for a Hypothetical Novel: An Address," reprinted in *Nobody Knows My Name*, in *James Baldwin: Collected Essays*, ed. Toni Morrison (New York: Library of America, 1998), 230.

4. *OED Online* (June 2020), s.v. "fake news, n.," https://www-oed-com.libproxy.wustl.edu/view/Entry/67776?redirectedFrom=fake+news#eid1264306660; Sarah Churchwell, *Behold, America: The Entangled History of "America First" and "the American Dream"* (New York: Basic, 2018), 42.

5. Churchwell, *Behold America*, 279.

6. Harry Frankfurt, *On Bullshit* (Princeton, NJ: Princeton University Press, 2005), 1.

7. For some discussion of this issue and several references to studies looking at divergence in attitudes toward race and gender in the U.S. electorate, see Thomas B. Edsall, "The Democratic Party Is Actually

Three Parties," *New York Times,* July 24, 2019, https://www.nytimes
.com/2019/07/24/opinion/2020-progressive-candidates.html.

8. Danielle Allen, *Talking to Strangers: Anxieties of Citizenship since
Brown v. Board of Education* (Chicago: University of Chicago Press,
2004), xxii.

9. Natalie Lira and Alexandra Minna Stern, "Mexican Americans and
Eugenic Sterilization: Resisting Reproductive Injustice in California,
1920–1950," *Aztlán: A Journal of Chicano Studies* 39, no. 2 (Fall 2014):
14, 15.

1. TRUTH

1. Frantz Fanon, *Black Skin, White Masks* (1952; new ed., New York:
Grove, 2008), xv.

2. Henry Louis Gates Jr. discusses these statistics in a short piece,
"How Many Slaves Landed in the U.S.?," https://www.theroot.com
/how-many-slaves-landed-in-the-us-1790873989. Steven Mintz,
"Historical Context: Facts about the Slave Trade and Slavery,"
Gilder Lehrman Institute of American History online, https://www
.gilderlehrman.org/content/historical-context-facts-about-slave
-trade-and-slavery; https://www.census.gov/library/publications
/1864/dec/1860a.html. The Trans-Atlantic Slave Trade Database is
here: https://www.slavevoyages.org.

3. Stephen R. Haynes, *Noah's Curse: The Biblical Justification of American Slavery* (New York: Oxford University Press, 2002).

4. The most thorough and comprehensive history of racist ideas in
American history is Ibram X. Kendi, *Stamped from the Beginning:
The Definitive History of Racist Ideas in America* (New York: Bold
Type, 2016).

5. Robin DiAngelo, *White Fragility: Why It's So Hard for White People
to Talk about Racism* (Boston: Beacon, 2018), 2.

6. Robert Tracy McKenzie, "'Revisionist' History," *Faith and History*
(blog), June 10, 2013, https://faithandamericanhistory.wordpress
.com/2013/06/10/revisionist-history/.

7. Gingrich quoted in Gary B. Nash, "The History Standards Controversy and Social History," *Journal of Social History* 29 (1995): 42.

8. See Abram C. Van Engen, *City on a Hill: A History of American*

Exceptionalism (New Haven, CT: Yale University Press, 2020). See also Daniel T. Rodgers, *As a City on a Hill: The Story of America's Most Famous Lay Sermon* (Princeton, NJ: Princeton University Press, 2018).

9. Morison and Commager quoted in Nash, "History Standards Controversy," 43. Direct reference: Samuel Eliot Morison and Henry Steele Commager, *The Growth of the American Republic*, vol. 1 (1930; New York: Oxford University Press, 1950), 537, 538, 539; italics added.

10. Morison and Commager, *The Growth of the American Republic*, 1:537. Note that the 1969 and 1980 editions changed much of this language; by 1969, although the volume still gave opinions from all sides on slavery, they do note, "Negro slavery in the South has been called the most oppressive and exploitative system of labor in history." (Immediately thereafter, the authors qualify this by noting, "It is often forgotten that the slave trade was begun by Negroes in Africa before Europeans reached the 'Dark Continent'" [1:472].) Also "pickaninnies" was changed to "children" (1:473), and there was a whole new section devoted to insurrections that took them much more seriously than did the 1930 edition. Textbook publishers were relying on the Dunning school of Reconstruction to reach for a white national unity, and reaching for that unity in the 1930s helped them sell textbooks both north and south.

11. Francis Butler Simkins, Spotswood Hunnicutt, and Sidman E. Poole, *Virginia: History, Government, Geography* (New York: Scribner's, 1957). Quoted in Adam Wesley Dean, "'Who Controls the Past Controls the Future': The Virginia History Textbook Controversy," *Virginia Magazine of History and Biography* 117, no. 4 (2009): 332; and Rex Springston, "Happy Slaves? The Peculiar Story of Three Virginia School Textbooks," *Richmond Times-Dispatch,* April 14, 2018, https://www.richmond.com/discover-richmond/happy-slaves -the-peculiar-story-of-three-virginia-school-textbooks/article_47 e79d49-eac8–575d-ac9d-1c6fce52328f.html.

12. Lynne Cheney, "The End of History," *Wall Street Journal,* October 20, 1994, http://www-personal.umich.edu/~mlassite/discussions 261/cheney.html. See also Gary B. Nash, "Lynne Cheney's Attack on the History Standards, 10 Years Later," https://historynewsnetwork .org/article/8418.

13. Peter N. Stearns, "Uncivil War: Current American Conservatives and Social History," *Journal of Social History* 29 (1995): 8, 9.

14. David S. Broder, "Dole Backs Official Language," *Washington Post,* September 5, 1995, A5, A1.

15. Dole quoted in B. Drummond Ayres Jr., "Dole Aims a Barrage at 'Intellectual Elites,'" *New York Times,* September 5, 1995, A15.

16. Broder, "Dole Backs Official Language," A5.

17. Alyson M. Cole, *The Cult of True Victimhood: From the War on Welfare to the War on Terror* (Stanford, CA: Stanford University Press, 2007), 6, 12, 9.

18. George Will, "Politics Permeates Too Many Campuses," *St. Louis Post-Dispatch,* September 16, 1990, 3B.

19. Dinesh D'Souza, *Illiberal Education: The Politics of Race and Sex on Campus* (New York: Free Press, 1991).

20. Nash, "History Standards Controversy," 44.

21. Joyce Appleby, Lynn Hunt, and Margaret Jacob, *Telling the Truth about History* (New York: Norton, 1994), 10, 11, 297, 274.

22. Lynne Cheney, *Telling the Truth: Why Our Culture and Our Country Have Stopped Making Sense—and What We Can Do about It* (New York: Simon and Schuster, 1995), 26.

23. Lynne Cheney, *We the People: The Story of Our Constitution* (New York: Simon and Schuster, 2008), 22, 24.

24. Cheney, *We the People,* 5.

25. Appleby, Hunt, and Jacob, *Telling the Truth about History,* 296, 297.

26. Michael Eric Dyson, foreword to DiAngelo, *White Fragility,* ix.

27. "Limbaugh: 'If Any Race of People Should Not Have Guilt about Slavery, It's Caucasians,'" video from July 22, 2013, cached by MediaMatters, https://www.mediamatters.org/video/2013/07/22/limbaugh-if-any-race-of-people-should-not-have/194999.

28. Jonathan Chait, "Why Rush Limbaugh Can't Stop Talking about Slavery," *New York Magazine,* October 6, 2014, http://nymag.com/intelligencer/2014/10/why-limbaugh-cant-stop-talking-about-slavery.html.

29. James Baldwin, "Words of a Native Son," in *James Baldwin: Collected Essays,* ed. Toni Morrison (New York: Library of America, 1998), 713. Note that this is a later essay than those appearing in Baldwin's 1955 collection *Notes of a Native Son.*

30. Baldwin, *The Fire Next Time* (1962; New York: Vintage, 1993), 8–9 (this excerpt was originally published in "Letter from a Region in My Mind," *New Yorker,* November 10, 1962).

31. DiAngelo, *White Fragility,* 103.

32. Glaude, *Begin Again,* 8–9.

33. DiAngelo, *White Fragility,* 59.

34. Appleby, Hunt, and Jacob, *Telling the Truth about History,* 295–96. Reassuring as this distorted memory may feel, Wendell Berry describes it as "the hidden wound," the injury that racism has inflicted upon white people themselves, though most can hardly bear to face it (Wendell Berry, *The Hidden Wound* [1989; Berkeley, CA: Counterpoint, 2019]; Fanon, *Black Skin, White Masks,* 205).

35. W. E. B. Du Bois, *Black Reconstruction in America,* introduced by David Levering Lewis (1935; New York: Free Press, 1992), 713, 722, 724, 723. Lewis's "revisionist masterpiece" evaluation is in his introduction to the work (vii). DuBois's book was a critique of the whole Dunning school at precisely the moment the Morison/Commager textbook cited above was in circulation.

36. Du Bois, *Black Reconstruction,* 725, 727 725, 728, 714.

37. James W. Loewen, *Lies My Teacher Told Me: Everything Your American History Textbook Got Wrong* (1995; New York: New Press, 2018), 142.

38. Southern Poverty Law Center, *Teaching Hard History: American Slavery* (2018), https://www.splcenter.org/sites/default/files /tt_hard_history_american_slavery.pdf, 9–10; Unwin quoted in Appleby, Hunt, and Jacob, *Telling the Truth about History,* 295.

39. Southern Poverty Law Center, *Teaching Hard History,* 10.

40. Kathleen Belew, *Bring the War Home: The White Power Movement and Paramilitary America* (Cambridge, MA: Harvard University Press, 2018).

41. Edward E. Baptist, *The Half Has Never Been Told: Slavery and the Making of American Capitalism* (New York: Basic, 2014), xxiii–xxiv.

42. Baptist, *Half Has Never Been Told,* xxv.

43. Caitlin Rosenthal, "The Perils of Big Data: How Crunching Numbers Can Lead to Moral Blunders," *Washington Post,* February 18, 2019, https://www.washingtonpost.com/outlook/2019/02/18/perils-big

-data-how-crunching-numbers-can-lead-moral-blunders/?utm
_term=.ece9f8e94ef6.

44. Baptist, *Half Has Never Been Told,* xxiii.

45. Loewen, *Lies My Teacher Told Me,* 140, xx.

46. Veronike Collazo, "For Black History Month, This Loudoun County Elementary School Played a Runaway Slave 'Game' in Gym Class," *Loudon Times-Mirror,* February 21, 2019, https://www.loudoun times.com/news/for-black-history-month-this-loudoun-county -elementary-school-played/article_9cecd568–35ef-11e9-8540-6372 d03d3025.html.

47. Jennifer Schuessler, "'A Fine Dessert': Judging a Book by the Smile of a Slave," *New York Times,* November 6, 2015, https://www .nytimes.com/2015/11/07/books/a-fine-dessert-judging-a-book-by -the-smile-of-a-slave.html; Allyson Criner Brown, "NOT Recom- mended: A Birthday Cake for George Washington," Teaching for Change, January 15, 2016, https://www.teachingforchange.org/gw -birthday-cake-not-recommended; Eyder Peralta, "Teaching Kids about Slavery: Picture Books Struggle with the Task," *All Things Considered,* NPR, January 22, 2016, https://www.npr.org/2016/01 /22/463977451/controversial-picture-books-surface-struggle-to -help-children-understand-slavery. *A Fine Dessert* featured cheerful scenes of an enslaved girl and her mother picking blackberries from the plantation garden and baking them into a pie for the master and family; *A Birthday Cake for George Washington* showed Washing- ton's enslaved chef and the chef's enslaved daughter happily baking the president's birthday cake together.

48. Charles W. Mills, *Black Rights/White Wrongs: The Critique of Racial Liberalism* (New York: Oxford University Press, 2017), 51, 49.

49. Jonathan Lemire, "Trump on Civil War: Why Couldn't They Have Worked That Out?" *AP News,* May 1, 2017, https://apnews.com /4d0e9994c6e445c689025e40a8a4308b; Christina Zhao, "Tucker Carlson Calls Concerns about White Supremacy a 'Hoax,'" *News- week,* August 6, 2019, https://www.newsweek.com/tucker-carlson -calls-concerns-about-white-supremacy-hoax-its-actually-not-real -problem-1452924.

50. Ronald Reagan, "Farewell Address to the Nation," January 11, 1989, https://www.reaganfoundation.org/media/128652/farewell.pdf.

51. "Transcript: Obama's Speech at Selma Marking 'Bloody Sunday,'" *Washington Post,* March 7, 2015, https://www.washington post.com/politics/transcript-obamas-speech-at-selma-marking -bloody-sunday-anniversary/2015/03/07/411d8eac-c4fc-11e4-ad5c -3b8ce89f1b89_story.html?utm_term=.700053615b09.

52. "Transcript: Obama's Speech at Selma," https://www.washington post.com/politics/transcript-obamas-speech-at-selma-marking -bloody-sunday-anniversary/2015/03/07/411d8eac-c4fc-11e4-ad5c -3b8ce89f1b89_story.html?utm_term=.700053615b09.

53. "Resistance to School Desegregation," Equal Justice Initiative, https://eji.org/history-racial-injustice-resistance-to-school -desegregation.

54. See Rebecca Bellan, "$23 Billion Education Funding Report Reveals Less Money for City Kids," CityLab, March 27, 2019, https://www .citylab.com/equity/2019/03/education-nonwhite-urban-school -districts-funding-tax/585691/.

55. Tim Naftali, "Ronald Reagan's Long-Hidden Racist Conversation with Richard Nixon," *Atlantic,* July 30, 2019, https://www .theatlantic.com/ideas/archive/2019/07/ronald-reagans-racist -conversation-richard-nixon/595102/; on "welfare queen," see Wahneema Lubiano, "Black Ladies, Welfare Queens, and State Minstrels: Ideological War by Narrative Means," in *Race-ing Justice, En-Gendering Power: Essays on Anita Hill, Clarence Thomas, and the Construction of Social Reality,* ed. Toni Morrison (New York: Pantheon, 1992), 323–63; and Premilla Nadasen, "From Widow to 'Welfare Queen': Welfare and the Politics of Race," *Black Women, Gender, and Families* 1, no. 2 (Fall 2007): 52–77.

56. Ian Haney López, *Dog Whistle Politics* (New York: Oxford University Press, 2014), 66, 70.

57. Danielle Allen, *Cuz: An American Tragedy* (New York: Liveright, 2018), 217–18.

58. Nikole Hannah-Jones, "What Is Owed," *New York Times Magazine,* June 30, 2020, https://www.nytimes.com/interactive/2020/06 /24/magazine/reparations-slavery.html. Hannah-Jones cites both studies: Christine Percheski and Christina Gibson-Davis, "A Penny on the Dollar: Racial Inequalities in Wealth among Households with Children," *Socius: Sociological Research for a Dynamic World*

6 (2020): 1–17: https://journals.sagepub.com/doi/pdf/10.1177/2378 023120916616; and Moritz Kuhn, Moritz Schularick, and Ulrike I. Steins, "Income and Wealth Inequality in America, 1949–2016," https://www.minneapolisfed.org/institute/working-papers -institute/iwp9.pdf (noted there to be forthcoming in the *Journal of Political Economy*).

59. "Ta-Nehisi Coates Makes the Case for Reparations," *Politico*, June 19, 2019, https://www.politico.com/video/2019/06/19/watch-ta-nehisi -coates-makes-the-case-for-reparations-068324; Coates, "The Case for Reparations," *Atlantic*, June 2014, https://www.theatlantic.com /magazine/archive/2014/06/the-case-for-reparations/361631/.

60. Mohamed Younis, "As Redress for Slavery, Americans Oppose Cash Reparations," Gallup, July 29, 2019, https://news.gallup.com/poll /261722/redress-slavery-americans-oppose-cash-reparations.aspx.

61. For a very brief overview, see Patricia Cohen, "What Reparations for Slavery Might Look Like in 2019," *New York Times*, May 23, 2019, https://www.nytimes.com/2019/05/23/business/economy /reparations-slavery.html. For a thorough and detailed account, see William A. Darity and A. Kristen Mullen, *From Here to Equality: Reparations for Black Americans in the Twenty-First Century* (Chapel Hill: University of North Carolina Press, 2020).

2. EMPATHY

1. William Cummings, "Outrage, Expressions of Support for Rep. Ilhan Omar after 'Send Her Back' Chant at Trump Rally," *USA Today*, July 18, 2019, https://www.usatoday.com/story/news/politics/2019/07/18 /ilhan-omar-send-her-back-chant-reactions/1764651001/.

2. Kevin Liptak and Sarah Westwood, "Trump Claims to Disavow Racists Chant after Pressure from Allies," *CNN Online*, July 18, 2019, https://www.cnn.com/2019/07/18/politics/trump-disavows-ilhan -omar-send-her-back-chant/index.html; Ilhan Omar, "It Is Not Enough to Condemn Trump's Racism," *New York Times*, July 25, 2019, https://www.nytimes.com/2019/07/25/opinion/ilhan-omar -trump-racism.html.

3. Donald J. Trump, Twitter post, July 14, 2019, 7:27 a.m., https:// twitter.com/realDonaldTrump/status/1150381395078000643.

4. Quoted in "Forgotten Ellis Island," https://www.youtube.com /watch?v=AuPZr68T_fg.

5. Dr. Alfred C. Reed, "The Medical Side of Immigration," *Popular Science Monthly* 80 (1912): 385, https://archive.org/stream /popularsciencemo80newyuoft/popularsciencemo80newyuoft _djvu.txt.

6. Lorie Conway, "Forgotten Ellis Island," Boston Film and Video Productions, 2011, https://www.youtube.com/watch?v=AuPZr68T_fg.

7. See Henry H. Goddard, "Mental Tests and the Immigrant," *Journal of Delinquency* 2, no. 5 (September 1917): 243–77, https://www .gwern.net/docs/iq/1917-goddard.pdf.

8. "The Immigration Act of 1924 (The Johnson-Reed Act)," Office of the Historian, U.S. Department of State, https://history.state.gov /milestones/1921–1936/immigration-act.

9. *Whom We Shall Welcome: Report of the President's Commission on Immigration and Naturalization* (Washington, DC: U.S. Government Printing Office, 1953), frontispiece, https://archive.org/stream /whomweshallwelco00unit#page/n5/mode/2up.

10. *Whom We Shall Welcome,* 108, 97 (the italicized text in the quotation appears in bold type in the source), https://archive.org/stream /whomweshallwelco00unit#page/108/mode/2up, https://archive .org/stream/whomweshallwelco00unit#page/96/mode/2up.

11. John F. Kennedy, *A Nation of Immigrants* (New York: Anti-Defamation League of B'nai B'rith, [1958]), 6, 26–27, 28.

12. Lyndon B. Johnson, quoted in Tom Gjelten, "In 1965, A Conservative Tried to Keep America White: His Plan Backfired," NPR, October 3, 2015, https://www.npr.org/2015/10/03/445339838/the-unintended -consequences-of-the-1965-immigration-act.

13. Tracy J. Davis, "Opening the Doors of Immigration: Sexual Orientation and Asylum in the United States," https://web.archive.org /web/20020822211541/http://www.wcl.american.edu/hrbrief/v6i3 /immigration.htm.

14. Needless to say, immigration statistics are contentious and highly political; for these, see Edwin S. Rubenstein, "Immigration Drives U.S. Population Growth," *NPG,* Negative Population Growth, Inc., January 2016, 1, https://npg.org/wp-content/uploads/2016/01/2016 -Immigration-Drives-Population-Forum-Paper.pdf.

15. "Modern Immigration Wave Brings 59 Million to U.S., Driving Population Growth and Change through 2065," Pew Research Center, September 28, 2015, http://www.pewhispanic.org/2015/09/28/modern-immigration-wave-brings-59-million-to-u-s-driving-population-growth-and-change-through-2065/.

16. Allan Smith, "Stephen Miller and Fox's Wallace Battle over Trump's National Emergency Declaration," NBC News, February 17, 2019, https://www.nbcnews.com/politics/donald-trump/stephen-miller-fox-s-wallace-battle-over-trump-s-national-n972596. The 27 percent figure comes from the Department of Homeland Security; see Michael Hoefer, Nancy Rytina, and Bryan C. Baker, *Estimates of the Unauthorized Immigrant Population Residing in the United States: January 2009* (Office of Immigration Studies, U.S. Department of Homeland Security, 2010), https://www.dhs.gov/sites/default/files/publications/Unauthorized%20Immigrant%20Population%20Estimates%20in%20the%20US%20January%202009.pdf.

17. Stephen Miller, quoted in Julie Hirschfeld Davis and Michael D. Shear, "How Trump Came to Enforce a Practice of Separating Migrant Families," *New York Times*, June 16, 2018, https://www.nytimes.com/2018/06/16/us/politics/family-separation-trump.html?module=inline.

18. Julia Ainsley, "Thousands More Migrant Kids Separated from Parents under Trump Than Previously Reported," NBC News, January 17, 2019, https://www.nbcnews.com/politics/immigration/thousands-more-migrant-kids-separated-parents-under-trump-previously-reported-n959791.

19. Elliot Spagat, "Tally of Children Split at Border Tops 5,400 in New Count," Associated Press, October 25, 2019, https://apnews.com/article/c654e652a4674cf19304a4a4ff599feb; Christopher Sherman, Martha Mendoza, and Garance Burke, "US Held Record Number of Migrant Children in Custody in 2019," Associated Press, November 12, 2019, https://apnews.com/article/015702afdb4d4fbf85cf5070cd2c6824.

20. Tara Zahra, "The Ugly U.S. History of Separating Families Goes Back Way beyond Trump," *Daily Beast,* August 3, 2018, https://www.thedailybeast.com/the-ugly-us-history-of-separating-families-goes-back-way-beyond-trump.

21. Austin Cannon, "Trump Says Mollie Tibbetts' Death 'Should've Never Happened,' Calls Immigration Laws 'a Disgrace,'" *Des Moines Register,* August 21, 2018, https://www.desmoinesregister.com /story/news/2018/08/21/mollie-tibbetts-missing-iowa-student -body-found-donald-trump-immigration/1058489002/; Natasha Koreck and Quint Forgey, "Trump's New Rallying Cry: Mollie Tibbets," *Politico,* August 22, 2018, https://www.politico.com/story /2018/08/22/mollie-tibbetts-death-donald-trump-791461. On recurring "invasion" language, see Jeremy W. Peters, Michael M. Grynbaum, Keith Collins, Rich Harris, and Rumsey Taylor, "How the El Paso Killer Echoed the Incendiary Words of Conservative Media Stars," *New York Times,* August 11, 2019, https://www.ny times.com/interactive/2019/08/11/business/media/el-paso-killer -conservative-media.html?action=click&module=Top%20Stories& pgtype=Homepage.

22. On Garrison, see Mitchell Sunderland, "The Anti-Vaxx Conspiracy Theorist Whose Cartoons Have Entranced Kylie Jenner," *Vice,* March 14, 2016, https://www.vice.com/en_us/article/wnwmyy /kylie-jenner-anti-vaxx-conspiracy-theory-tweet; Emma Grey Ellis, "The Alt-Right Found Its Favorite Cartoonist—and Almost Ruined His Life," *Wired,* June 19, 2017, https://www.wired.com/story/ben -garrison-alt-right-cartoonist/; and Garrison's own website: https:// grrrgraphics.com.

23. Jonathan Blitzer, "Donald Trump, the Migrant Caravan, and a Manu-factured Crisis at the U.S. Border," *New Yorker,* November 14, 2018, https://www.newyorker.com/news/news-desk/donald-trump-the -migrant-caravan-and-a-manufactured-crisis-at-the-us-border. Garri-son's cartoons are available at https://www.grrrgraphics.com/cartoons.

24. https://www.washingtonpost.com/world/2018/11/26/how -photographer-captured-image-migrant-mother-her-children -fleeing-tear-gas/?utm_term=.d83570e0ea3b.

25. Michael J. Mooney, *Texas Monthly,* August 2019, https://www.texas monthly.com/articles/donald-trump-defender-dallas-pastor-robert -jeffress/.

26. Matthew Schmalz, "What the Bible Says about Welcoming Refu-gees," *The Conversation,* January 29, 2017, https://theconversation .com/what-the-bible-says-about-welcoming-refugees-72050.

27. Matthew 25:31–40 (New Revised Standard Version).

28. *Stanford Encyclopedia of Philosophy,* s.v. "Empathy," https://plato
.stanford.edu/entries/empathy/.

29. Paul Bloom, *Against Empathy: The Case for Rational Compassion*
(New York: HarperCollins, 2016), 16.

30. Bloom, *Against Empathy,* 34, 31.

31. Elizabeth N. Simas, Scott Clifford, and Justin H. Kirkland,
"How Empathic Concern Fuels Political Polarization," *American
Political Science Review,* October 31, 2019, 1, 2, 1, 3, https://www
.cambridge.org/core/journals/american-political-science-review
/article/how-empathic-concern-fuels-political-polarization
/8115DB5BDE548FF6AB04DA661F83785E.

32. Jason Marsh, "The Limits of David Brooks' 'Limits of Empathy,'"
Greater Good Magazine, October 4, 2011, https://greatergood
.berkeley.edu/article/item/the_limits_of_david_brooks_limits_of
_empathy.

33. See C. Daniel Batson, *Altruism in Humans* (New York: Oxford University Press, 2011).

34. Marsh, "Limits."

35. For a very brief overview of this debate and links to a few other
relevant sources, see not only Bloom but also Roman Krznaric,
"Welcome to the Empathy Wars," *Open Democracy,* June 29, 2015,
https://www.opendemocracy.net/en/transformation/welcome-to
-empathy-wars/.

36. Barack Obama, "DNC 2004 Keynote Address," July 27, 2004, http://
cultureofempathy.com/Obama/SpeechIndex.htm#2004–11-XX%20
-%20Sen.%20Barack%20Obama%20-%20O%20Magazine.

37. Obama, "U. Massachusetts Boston Commencement," full text
available at https://www.youtube.com/watch?v=bwaoeVPcOW4&
feature=youtu.be&t=31.

3. COURAGE

1. Silvia M. Dutchevici, quoted in Jen Kim, "Are Female Misogynists
on the Rise?," *Psychology Today,* October 25, 2016, https://www
.psychologytoday.com/us/blog/valley-girl-brain/201610/are-female
-misogynists-the-rise.

2. Kate Manne, *Down Girl: The Logic of Misogyny* (New York: Oxford University Press, 2018), 64, 63; italics in original.

3. See Tom Goldman, https://www.npr.org/2019/08/08/747766451 /after-world-cup-win-other-u-s-womens-sports-leagues-ask-what -about-us; Darcy Lockman, *All the Rage: Mothers, Fathers, and the Myth of Equal Partnership* (New York: HarperCollins, 2019).

4. Manne, *Down Girl*, 69, 72, 197.

5. Manne, *Down Girl*, 291.

6. Tomi Lahren, Twitter post, July 31, 2019, 7:26 p.m., https://twitter .com/tomilahren/status/1156722853846237184?lang=en.

7. Amanda Hess, "'Ditsy, Predatory White House Intern': Looking Back on How Maureen Dowd Painted Monica Lewinsky as a Crazy Bimbo—and Won a Pulitzer for It," *Slate.com,* May 7, 2014, https:// slate.com/human-interest/2014/05/monica-lewinsky-returns-how -maureen-dowd-caricatured-bill-clintons-mistress-as-a-crazy -bimbo.html.

8. See Elizabeth Reis, *Damned Women: Sinners and Witches in Puritan New England* (Ithaca, NY: Cornell University Press, 1997).

9. Abigail Adams to John Adams, March 31, 1776, and John Adams to Abigail Adams, April 14, 1776, Adams Family Correspondence, volume 1, Adams Papers Digital Edition, Massachusetts Historical Society, http://www.masshist.org/publications/adams-papers /index.php/view/ADMS-04-01-02-0241 and http://www.masshist .org/publications/adams-papers/index.php/view/ADMS-04-01-02 -0248.

10. Reva B. Siegel, "The Modernization of Marital Status Law: Adjudicating Wives' Rights to Earnings, 1860–1930," *Georgetown Law Journal* 82 (1993–94): 2129.

11. Catherine Allgor, "Coverture: The Word You Probably Don't Know But Should," *National Women's History Museum,* September 4, 2014, https://www.womenshistory.org/articles/coverture-word -you-probably-dont-know-should?fbclid=IwAR1h4PLFjT4o5 S7oUwn3MHO9GW6maImp30J2JyTnVls3wB3f6ewq5RktjKA#.X URbVqH5bVA.facebook.

12. Anzia Yezierska, *Bread Givers,* 3rd ed., foreword and introduction by Alice Kessler-Harris (1925; New York: Persea, 2003), 206, 9–10, 296.

13. Robert Anthony Orsi, *The Madonna of 115th Street: Faith and Community in Italian Harlem, 1880–1950,* 2nd ed. (1985; New Haven, CT: Yale University Press, 2002), 144–45.

14. Evelyn Brooks Higginbotham, *Righteous Discontent: The Women's Movement in the Black Baptist Church, 1880–1920* (Cambridge, MA: Harvard University Press, 1993), 151; Moya Bailey and Trudy, "On Misogynoir: Citation, Erasure, and Plagiarism," *Feminist Media Studies,* 18, no. 4, 2018, 762–68, DOI: 10.1080/14680777.2018 .1447395.

15. Frances Ellen Watkins Harper, "We Are All Bound up Together," address to the Eleventh National Women's Rights Convention, May 1, 1866, https://awpc.cattcenter.iastate.edu/2017/03/21/we-are-all -bound-up-together-may-1866/.

16. Quoted in Marjorie Spruill Wheeler, *New Women of the New South: The Leaders of the Woman Suffrage Movement in the Southern States* (New York: Oxford University Press, 1993), 26, 25, 26.

17. Artwork by Laura E. Foster, ca. 1912, published in *Life Magazine,* August 22, 1912. From the collections of the Library of Congress (https://www.loc.gov/item/2002716765/).

18. On the history of African American women's fight for suffrage and women's rights, see Martha S. Jones, *Vanguard: How Black Women Broke Barriers, Won the Vote, and Insisted on Equality for All* (New York: Basic, 2020); on the history of attempts at Black disenfranchisement into our own time, see Carol Anderson, *One Person, No Vote: How Voter Suppression Is Destroying Our Democracy* (New York: Bloomsbury, 2018).

19. Was it mere coincidence that Curtis was partly Native American and an enrolled member of the Kaw tribe, spending many of his growing-up years on a Kaw Indian reservation in Kansas? Either way, of him a Washington correspondent wrote that feminists "called him a friend, and it is one of the proudest of his claims that he led the floor fight for the Nineteenth Amendment" ("Charles Curtis, 31st Vice President [1929–1933]," United States Senate, https://www.senate .gov/artandhistory/history/common/generic/VP_Charles_Curtis .htm).

20. Jane J. Mansbridge, *Why We Lost the ERA* (Chicago: University of Chicago Press, 1986), 8.

21. Sanger quoted in "Hayes Denounces Birth Control Aim," *New York Times*, November 21, 1921, 6. See R. Marie Griffith, *Moral Combat: How Sex Divided American Christians and Fractured American Politics* (New York: Basic, 2017), 14–28. Indeed, one of the reasons so many people today are convinced that Sanger was nothing but an evil eugenicist intent on murdering Black babies—which is completely false—is because some Catholic leaders focused enormous attention on her for years and inspired several right-wing Catholic writers to write deceitful, scathing books about her that have been widely cited and circulated and contain numerous falsehoods.

22. See Dorothy Roberts's nuanced discussion of Sanger, eugenics, and racism in *Killing the Black Body: Race, Reproduction, and the Meaning of Liberty* (1997; New York: Vintage, 2016), 76–79; see also Imani Gandy, "How False Narratives of Margaret Sanger Are Being Used to Shame Black Women," *Rewire.News*, August 20, 2015, https://rewire .news/article/2015/08/20/false-narratives-margaret-sanger-used -shame-black-women/.

23. Claudia Goldin and Claudia Olivetti, "Shocking Labor Supply: A Reassessment of the Role of World War II on Women's Labor Supply," *American Economic Review: Papers and Proceedings* 103, no. 3 (2013): 257, https://scholar.harvard.edu/files/goldin/files/goldin -olivetti_paper.pdf.

24. Daron Acemoglu, David Autor, and David Lyle, "Women, War and Wages: The Effect of Female Labor Supply on the Wage Structure at Mid-Century," NBER Working Paper No. 9013, National Bureau of Economic Research, June 2002, 2, https://www.nber.org/papers /w9013.pdf.

25. *The Phyllis Schlafly Report* 5, no. 7 (February 1972): n.p., cited in Katherine Kraft, "ERA: History and Status," *Radcliffe Quarterly* 68, no. 1 (March 1982): 6.

26. Mansbridge, *Why We Lost the ERA*, 69.

27. Charles Colson, "The Thomas Hearings and the New Gender Wars," *Christianity Today*, November 25, 1991, 72; Rush H. Limbaugh III, *The Way Things Ought to Be* (New York: Pocket Books 1992), 115; Felicity Barringer, "One Year Later, Anita Hill Interprets Thomas Hearings," *New York Times*, October 17, 1992, 6, https://www.ny times.com/1992/10/17/us/one-year-later-anita-hill-interprets

-thomas-hearings.html; Joe Holley, "Rosalie Silberman, Created Independent Women's Forum," *Washington Post,* February 21, 2007, B6, https://www.washingtonpost.com/archive/local/2007/02/21 /rosalie-silberman/1dba8e76-ea4d-4a49-b5a8-5f070b521a4e/.

28. "Hillary's First Joint Interview—Next to Bill in '92," *60 Minutes Overtime,* February 1, 2013, https://www.cbsnews.com/news /hillarys-first-joint-interview-next-to-bill-in-92/; https://www .politico.com/magazine/story/2016/09/hillary-clinton-2016-60 -minutes-1992-214275.

29. Monica Lewinsky, "Shame and Survival," *Vanity Fair,* May 28, 2014, https://www.vanityfair.com/style/society/2014/06/monica -lewinsky-humiliation-culture; Lewinsky, "The Price of Shame," Ted2015, https://www.ted.com/talks/monica_lewinsky_the_price _of_shame?language=en#t-670650.

30. I recount these stories in detail in Griffith, *Moral Combat,* 241–72. Since that book's publication, a new foreword to *Strange Justice* written by Jill Abramson offers new evidence supporting Hill's account of Thomas's behavior (Jill Abramson, "Foreword: Do You Believe Her Now?," in Jane Mayer and Jill Abramson, *Strange Justice: The Selling of Clarence Thomas* [1994; New York: Graymalkin Media, 2018], xi–xxiii). Clinton's payment of an $850,000 settlement to Jones adds credence to most Americans' belief that Jones was telling the truth, despite Clinton's refusal to apologize or acknowledge it.

31. Cole, *Cult of True Victimhood,* 47, 49.

32. All quotes from Cole, *Cult of True Victimhood,* 48, 49, 50.

33. Elizabeth Fox-Genovese, *"Feminism Is Not the Story of My Life": How Today's Feminist Elite Has Lost Touch with the Real Concerns of Women* (New York: Doubleday, 1995), 163, 145.

34. Kate Manne, Twitter post, August 4, 2019, 10:02 p.m., https://twitter .com/kate_manne/status/1158211528383959040.

35. This is an inadequate discussion of transmisogyny, but the controversies over nonexpert scholars writing about trans issues are acute at the time of writing, such that I do not feel equipped with the expertise to treat this subject with the depth it deserves. See the very brief discussion of transmisogyny in Manne, *Down Girl,* 24–25; as well as Julia Serano, *Whipping Girl: A Transsexual Woman on*

Sexism and the Scapegoating of Femininity (2007; 2nd ed., Berkeley, CA: Seal, 2016).

36. Sarah Pulliam Bailey, "The Deep Disgust for Hillary Clinton That Drives So Many Evangelicals to Support Trump," *Washington Post,* October 9, 2016, https://www.washingtonpost.com/news/acts-of -faith/wp/2016/10/09/the-deep-disgust-for-hillary-clinton-that -drives-so-many-evangelicals-to-support-trump/.

37. Anna North, "Trump Adviser's Slur Is a Sign of Things to Come," *New York Times,* November 2, 2016, https://www.nytimes.com/2016 /11/02/opinion/the-power-of-anti-hillary-slurs.html.

38. Proverbs 5:5 (New Revised Standard Version). All of these sayings, shirts, and buttons are shown in rally photographs from two articles: Claire Landsbaum, "The Most Misogynistic Gear Spotted at Trump Rallies," *New York,* October 12, 2016, https://www.thecut.com/2016 /10/the-most-misogynistic-things-people-wore-to-trump-rallies .html; and Michelle Goldberg and Chelsea Hassler, "A Children's Treasury of Misogyny at the Republican National Convention," *Slate,* July 20, 2016, https://slate.com/news-and-politics/2016/07/misogyny -is-alive-and-well-at-the-republican-national-convention.html.

39. "An Examination of the 2016 Electorate, Based on Validated Voters," Pew Research Center, August 9, 2018, https://www.pewresearch.org /politics/2018/08/09/an-examination-of-the-2016-electorate-based -on-validated-voters/.

40. Corky Siemaszko, "U.S. Abortion Rate Now at Lowest Level It's Been since *Roe v. Wade,*" NBC News online, January 17, 2017, https:// www.nbcnews.com/news/us-news/u-s-abortion-rate-now-lowest -level-it-s-been-n707791.

41. Kate Manne, "Forum: The Logic of Misogyny," *Boston Review,* July 11, 2016, http://bostonreview.net/forum/kate-manne-logic -misogyny.

42. Jia Tolentino, "Republicans Offer a Shocking Defense: Sexual Assault Isn't a Big Deal," *New Yorker,* September 20, 2018, https:// www.newyorker.com/news/our-columnists/after-the-kavanaugh -allegations-republicans-offer-a-shocking-defense-sexual-assault -isnt-a-big-deal.

43. Billy Sherrill and Tammy Wynette, "Stand by Your Man," https:// www.azlyrics.com/lyrics/tammywynette/standbyyourman.html.

44. Per Bauhn, *The Value of Courage* (Lund, Sweden: Nordic Academic Press, 2003), 9, 32.

45. Slavoj Žižek, *The Courage of Hopelessness: Chronicles of a Year of Acting Dangerously* (London: Penguin, 2018), xi–xii.

4. CONVERSATION

1. See Melanie McFarland, "CNN and NBC Betray Sunday Viewers Seeking Analysis on Damning Climate Change Report," *Salon,* November 26, 2018, https://www.salon.com/2018/11/26/cnn-and -nbc-betray-sunday-viewers-seeking-analysis-on-damning-climate -change-report/; Kenneth Boyd, "Bothsidesism and Why It Matters," *Prindle Post,* January 2, 2019, https://www.prindlepost.org /2019/01/bothsidesism-and-why-it-matters/.

2. Lutz Kaelber, "Eugenics: Compulsory Sterilization in 50 American States," https://www.uvm.edu/~lkaelber/eugenics/.

3. Natalie Lira and Alexandra Minna Stern, "Mexican Americans and Eugenic Sterilization: Resisting Reproductive Injustice in California, 1920–1950," *Aztlán: A Journal of Chicano Studies* 39, no. 2 (Fall 2014): 13; Lutz Kaelber, "Eugenics/Eugenic Sterilizations in Indiana," https://www.uvm.edu/~lkaelber/eugenics/IN/IN.html.

4. Kaelber, "Eugenics," "California," https://www.uvm.edu/~lkaelber /eugenics/CA/CA.html.

5. Lira and Stern, "Mexican Americans and Eugenic Sterilization," 14, 15.

6. Quoted in Lira and Stern, "Mexican Americans and Eugenic Sterilization," 16.

7. Lira and Stern, "Mexican Americans and Eugenic Sterilization," 26.

8. Kathleen M. Sands, *America's Religious Wars: The Embattled Heart of Our Public Life* (New Haven, CT: Yale University Press, 2019), 7.

9. Douglas Laycock, afterword to *Same-Sex Marriage and Religious Liberty: Emerging Conflicts,* ed. Douglas Laycock, Anthony R. Picarello Jr., and Robin Fretwell Wilson (Lanham, MD: Rowman and Littlefield, 2008), 190–91.

10. Laycock, afterword to *Same-Sex Marriage and Religious Liberty,* 191, 194.

11. Amy Gutmann and Dennis Thompson, *Why Deliberative Democracy?* (Princeton, NJ: Princeton University Press, 2004), 74. As they write: "The core of the problem is not merely that people disagree,

but that some of the disagreement is reasonable. It is built into the circumstances of social and political life. When citizens disagree about such issues as the morality of abortion, capital punishment, starting a preventive war, or funding health care, deliberation does not produce agreement, and perhaps even should not" (14).

12. Douglas Laycock, "Religious Liberty and the Culture Wars," *University of Illinois Law Review* (2014): 866, 869, http://illinoislawreview.org/wp-content/ilr-content/articles/2014/3/Laycock.pdf.

13. Douglas Laycock, "Religious Liberty, Health Care, and the Culture Wars," in *Law, Religion, and Health in the United States,* ed. Holly Fernandez Lynch, I. Glenn Cohen, and Elizabeth Sepper (New York: Cambridge University Press, 2017), 33.

14. Amy Gais, *Bound by Belief: Rethinking Liberty of Conscience in Early Modern Political Thought* (forthcoming).

15. *Trapped,* dir. Dawn Porter, film (Trilogy Films, 2016). The first scene starts around 52:38 and the second at 53:30.

16. "Should We Tolerate Evil Opinions?—Robert George on Peter Singer, Abortion, and Seeking Truth," *The Table,* September 12, 2015, https://cct.biola.edu/tolerate-evil-opinions-robert-george-peter-singer-abortion-seeking-truth/.

17. Robert P. George, Twitter post, June 28, 2019, 5:22 p.m., https://twitter.com/McCormickProf/status/1144732854527639554. See also David French's retort to pro-choice arguments that abortion foes care more about the fetus than living children or else they'd want higher taxes for child welfare: "The true concern [of the pro-choicer] isn't for child welfare but for transient notions of adult fulfillment, and no level of taxation will cure the selfishness of the human heart" (David French, "You're Not Really Pro-Life Unless You Support Higher Taxes," *National Review,* July 31, 2015: https://www.nationalreview.com/corner/youre-not-really-pro-life-unless-you-support-higher-taxes-david-french/).

18. Charles C. Camosy, *Beyond the Abortion Wars: A Way Forward for a New Generation* (Grand Rapids, MI: William B. Eerdmans, 2015), 13, 14, 161, 151. It is worth noting that Camosy co-organized and participated in a remarkable conference in which thinkers and activists across all sides of the abortion debate sought deep engagement and conversation with one another, "Open Hearts, Open Minds, and Fair Minded Words," held at Princeton University in 2010. His co-

organizers were the philosopher Peter Singer, Catholic reproductive rights activist Frances Kissling, and bioethicist Jennifer Miller. Notably, Robert George (a member of the Princeton faculty who was one of the university's most prominent public voices on abortion) did not attend; according to Kissling, "George was invited and refused" (Frances Kissling, email to author, October 12, 2020). On the conference, see Samantha Pergadia, "Seeking Common Ground," *Princeton Alumni Weekly,* November 17, 2010, https://paw.princeton.edu/article/seeking-common-ground.

19. Camosy, *Beyond the Abortion Wars,* 157; italics in the original.

20. Kate Greasley, *Arguments about Abortion: Personhood, Morality, and Law* (Oxford: Oxford University Press, 2017), 119.

21. Roger Wertheimer, "Understanding the Abortion Argument," *Philosophy and Public Affairs* 7 (1971): 3–74; quoted in Greasley, *Arguments about Abortion,* 105.

22. Greasley, *Arguments about Abortion,* 106. According to her footnotes, Greasley is specifically engaging here with Robert P. George and Christopher Tollefsen, *Embryo: A Defense of Human Life* (New York: Doubleday, 2008); Camosy, *Beyond the Abortion Wars,* 51.

23. Cathleen Kaveny, *Law's Virtues: Fostering Autonomy and Solidarity in American Society* (Washington, DC: Georgetown University Press, 2012), 5–6.

24. Marie Griffith, "Roe v. Wade at 40: An Interview with Legal Scholar and Theologian Cathleen Kaveny," *Religion & Politics,* January 23, 2013, https://religionandpolitics.org/2013/01/23/roe-v-wade-at-40-an-interview-with-legal-scholar-and-theologian-cathleen-kaveny/.

25. Dorothy Roberts, *Killing the Black Body: Race, Reproduction, and the Meaning of Liberty,* 2nd ed. (1997; New York: Vintage, 2017), xiv, xv.

26. *Trapped,* dir. Porter, film. This scene occurs around 1:01:55.

27. Katha Pollitt, *PRO: Reclaiming Abortion Rights* (New York: Picador, 2014), 71. Obviously, it is not Pollitt's intent to offer a judicious ethical rebuttal to the Catholic position; but if she's really trying to reach the "muddled middle," as she claims, cavalier sneering—even toward the sneer-ers, as I've already shown George to be—seems a poor tack.

28. Molly Jong-Fast, Twitter post, February 28, 2019, 1:43 p.m., https://twitter.com/MollyJongFast/status/1101206288204292096.

29. Lady Parts Justice, "Life Is a Living Nightmare: A Telethon to Fix It," February 1, 2018, https://ladypjustice.com/aiovg_videos/life-is-a-living-nightmare-a-telethon-to-fix-it/.

30. The classic analysis by this name remains powerfully relevant; see James C. Scott, *Weapons of the Weak: Everyday Forms of Peasant Resistance* (New Haven, CT: Yale University Press, 1987).

31. Frances Kissling, "Abortion Rights Are under Attack, and Pro-Choice Advocates Are Caught in a Time Warp," *Washington Post,* February 18, 2011, https://www.washingtonpost.com/opinions/a-pro-choice-choice-shift-course-or-lose-ground/2011/02/18/ABxaHSQ_story.html; cited in Camosy, *Beyond the Abortion Wars,* 39–40.

32. Arlene Carmen and Howard Moody, *Abortion Counseling and Social Change: From Illegal Act to Medical Practice* (Valley Forge, PA: Judson, 1973), 18–19, 19.

33. Joshua D. Wolff, "Ministers of a Higher Law: The Story of the Clergy Consultation Service on Abortion" (B.A. thesis, Amherst College, 1998); Cynthia S. Bumb to *St. Louis Post-Dispatch,* January 22, 1998, B (cited in Wolff, "Ministers of a Higher Law," 3).

34. Frances Kissling, interview by Rebecca Sharpless, transcript of audio recording, September 13–14, 2002, Population and Reproductive Health Oral History Project, Sophia Smith Collection, Smith College, 16, 37, 38, 56–57.

35. Traci Blackmon quoted in Hans Holznagel, "Religious Pro-Choice Stance: Not New to UCC, but Urgent as Ever," *United Church of Christ News,* May 22, 2019, https://www.ucc.org/religious_pro_choice_stance_not_new_to_ucc_but_urgent_as_ever_05212019.

36. Dr. Willie Parker, *Life's Work: A Moral Argument for Choice* (New York: Atria, 2017), 12–13, 116, 117.

37. Parker, *Life's Work,* 145, 146, 118, 158. It needs noting that a cloud has come to hang over Parker's abortion work, rightly or wrongly, for in 2019, a colleague accused Parker of sexual assault. Her accusation was not thoroughly investigated and has been called into question, and he has persistently denied the allegation; nonetheless, some of his allies in the abortion rights movement have distanced themselves from him. For those interested in a fair and nuanced accounting of the allegation and his response, see Maggie Bullock,

"The #MeToo Case That Divided the Abortion-Rights Movement,"
Atlantic, March 2020, https://www.theatlantic.com/magazine
/archive/2020/03/the-abortion-doctor-and-his-accuser/605578/.

38. Kira Schlesinger, *Pro-Choice and Christian: Reconciling Faith, Politics, and Justice* (Louisville, KY: Westminster John Knox, 2017), 87, 88.

39. Parker, *Life's Work,* 177; Schlesinger, *Pro-Choice and Christian,* 89, 119.

CONCLUSION

1. A classic analysis of this bunching phenomenon is Bill Bishop, *The Big Sort: Why the Clustering of Like-Minded America Is Tearing Us Apart* (New York: Houghton Mifflin Harcourt, 2008).

2. Loewen, *Lies My Teacher Told Me,* xix.

3. Commission on the Practice of Democratic Citizenship, *Our Common Purpose: Reinventing American Democracy for the 21st Century* (Cambridge, MA: American Academy of Arts & Sciences, 2020). Available in print form or online: https://www.amacad.org/sites /default/files/publication/downloads/2020-Democratic-Citizenship _Our-Common-Purpose_0.pdf. I'm grateful to Danielle Allen for asking me, early in the Commission's work, to write up a memo on "Rebuilding Shared Values," a project that greatly helped me think about the values highlighted in the essays here.

4. Molly Farneth, *Hegel's Social Ethics: Religion, Conflict, and Rituals of Reconciliation* (Princeton, NJ: Princeton University Press, 2017), 119. As Farneth writes, "Part of what makes democracy distinctive is the expectation that the government owes the people accountability of this sort." Cited in Fannie Bialek, "Optimism and Accountability: On Failing to Learn from Wounds," paper presented to the Workshop in Politics, Ethics, and Society, Washington University in St. Louis, November 1, 2019, 16, 18.

5. Michiko Kakutani, "The Handmaid's Thriller: In 'The Testaments,' There's a Spy in Gilead," *New York Times,* September 3, 2019, https:// www.nytimes.com/2019/09/03/books/review/testaments-margaret -atwood-handmaids-tale.html.

INDEX

ABOUT THE RICHARD E. MYERS LECTURES

The Richard E. Myers Lecture Series, hosted by University Baptist Church of Charlottesville, Virginia, presents world-class scholars with the opportunity to share their research with the Charlottesville community. The volume you now hold derives from this lecture series. Each volume represents a unique partnership between the academy and the church. The authors are not compelled to write within the constraints of any specific doctrine or dogma; they are free to write about what their research dictates. Through a public presentation and discussion, the authors develop their ideas into a contribution to historical and theological discourse. The ecclesial benefit traces its roots to Anselm's *fides quaerens intellectum,* and we hope this series continues the conversation of "faith seeking understanding" into the future.

An anonymous benefactor made the lectures and this book possible. The benefactor wanted a broad and inclusive series focused on contemporary theological issues, and she worked with the church in arranging the lectures and their publication. Thus, University Baptist Church is grateful for the partnership with the University of Virginia Press to publish this series.

Richard E. Myers, the namesake for the lecture series, served as the Senior Minister at University Baptist Church from 1964 to

1986. He tried throughout his ministry to recapture the mission and excitement of the early church while addressing the challenges facing contemporary Christians. Reverend Myers led the church through the tumultuous civil rights era, worked for open and fair housing, and sought to break down the barriers of racial segregation. The benefactor chose to honor his ministry with this series.

MATTHEW TENNANT, SERIES EDITOR

Charlottesville, Virginia